T0295816

PRAISE FOR *EMPLOYEE-GENERATED LEARNING*

Since implementing the *Employee-generated Learning* approach, weve gained almost 2000 content creators in our organization. While some are L&D people, the majority are regular employees – subject matter experts – who wouldnt have contributed without EGL.
Frédéric Hebert, Head of Digital Learning, Danone

In an era where the pace of change is relentless, this book is a must-read for L&D leaders. It provides a holistic, future-focused blueprint for L&D strategy, paving the way for a dynamic, knowledge-rich organizational culture.
Louise Puddifoot, L&D expert, Founder and Managing Director, Willow & Puddifoot

This book charts the twisting road from top-down formal learning to something more organic and emergent. It is an important journey that most learning organizations will have to travel. The book shows you why this is necessary and, more importantly, how to take the first steps and transform your whole L&D operation. It is not just about process; it is a whole new way of thinking and organizing. The ideas in this book are central to creating a more empowered and dynamic workforce, and more resilient organizations. Nothing is more important as far as I am concerned.
Nigel Paine, Co-Presenter of Learning Now TV

Learning is the fuel that powers successful organizations. Making it easy for subject matter experts across the organization to create and share knowledge is key in a world where change is happening faster than ever. Kasper and Videhis book is a must-read for anyone looking to leverage the knowledge across their people to develop training that drives performance and delivers results.
Brendan Noud, Co-founder and CEO, LearnUpon

Employee-generated Learning delivers valuable insights for L&D professionals to stay relevant in the ever-shifting world of work, including very practical ideas that we should all incorporate into our L&D strategies. Kasper and Videhis compelling narrative outlines the evolution of corporate learning over the past decades, highlighting parallels with other industries and drawing lessons from them to replace the outdated pedagogy of our industry. I, for one, will revisit this as my new team and organization develop its approaches around community-based learning. I highly recommend this book to all fellow professionals in L&D and people development.
Malcolm Taylor, Head of Capability, UK Health Security Agency.

A defining characteristic of a true learning culture is that leaders and experts are equipped and empowered to contribute to the learning of others in formal and informal ways – this is not solely the responsibility of L&D teams. In this book, Kasper and Videhi outline an approach and a process of how to effectively establish Employee-generated Learning as an impactful and practical way of scaling and speeding up the design the delivery of learning content. Overall, a powerful value proposition for EGL.
Thor Flosason, Ph.D., Head of Global Talent Management & Learning Operations, PepsiCo

This book reveals the importance of social learning in shaping an organizations culture. It deftly explores new ways of working with AI, advocating for innovation while maintaining a watchful eye. It is an insightful guide for organizations navigating the intersections of technology and collective learning.
Cecilie Tystad, Training Director Sales & Service for Europe, Electrolux

Employee-generated Learning

*How to develop training that
drives performance*

Kasper Spiro and Videhi Bhamidi

KoganPage

Publisher's note

Every possible effort has been made to ensure that the information contained in this book is accurate at the time of going to press, and the publishers and authors cannot accept responsibility for any errors or omissions, however caused. No responsibility for loss or damage occasioned to any person acting, or refraining from action, as a result of the material in this publication can be accepted by the editor, the publisher or the author.

First published in Great Britain and the United States in 2024 by Kogan Page Limited

2nd Floor, 45 Gee Street	8 W 38th Street, Suite 902	4737/23 Ansari Road
London	New York, NY 10018	Daryaganj
EC1V 3RS	USA	New Delhi 110002
United Kingdom		India

www.koganpage.com

Kogan Page books are printed on paper from sustainable forests.

ISBNs

Hardback   978 1 3986 1319 5
Paperback 978 1 3986 1317 1
Ebook   978 1 3986 1318 8

British Library Cataloguing-in-Publication Data

A CIP record for this book is available from the British Library.

Library of Congress Control Number
2023952593

Typeset by Integra Software Services, Pondicherry
Print production managed by Jellyfish
Printed and bound by CPI Group (UK) Ltd, Croydon, CR0 4YY

CONTENTS

ABOUT THE AUTHORS

Kasper Spiro is the Co-founder of and Chief Learning Strategist at Easygenerator, where he held the CEO position for 11 years. He is now responsible for the company's vision and direction. Easygenerator is an e-learning authoring tool that helps subject matter experts capture their knowledge and share it with their coworkers by providing an intuitive, easy-to-use environment. Kasper's background includes teaching, authoring textbooks, designing e-learning and developing software solutions for knowledge management, user performance support and e-learning. He is an international speaker, e-learning blogger, podcast host and author at many learning and development platforms.

Videhi Bhamidi is the Director of Research at Easygenerator and leads research studies to provide relevant insights to the Product, Customer Success, Sales, and Growth Marketing teams. She is an Oxford University graduate with a dual master's in education and human resources management, specializing in social, mobile and blended learning methods in corporate and government settings. Her works, including industry articles and academic research papers, have been published in multiple international publications. Videhi is a strong advocate for the power of education and believes in democratizing learning models to eliminate access barriers and make it more inclusive to all.

LIST OF CONTRIBUTORS

Sera Özkıvanç

Ines Pinto

Henan Rehman

Joni Toonen

Geert de Jong

Theresa Dada

Nigel Paine

Vasudha Chowdhary

Madhavi Tanikella

Joe Ferner-Reeves

Zexna Opara

Louise Puddifoot

Heather Gilmartin

FOREWORD

Suppose an organization knew what it didn't know, what a great source of growth it would be. But how do you get that knowledge to the surface? The larger the organization, the more complex the question becomes. Traditionally, it's been the boss's role to tell employees how things are done. But is that also the case with knowledge?

Knowledge becomes obsolete faster and faster these days. What was considered state of the art yesterday may not be so today. I work with start-ups and scale-ups, and when I walk into these environments – even with my decades-long experience – I often learn more than I contribute.

This book is about unleashing the hidden power of organizations. It introduces the concept of Employee-generated Learning and explains how you can implement it to create a culture of knowledge sharing. We invest a lot of money in knowledge and innovation, and rightly so. If you want to enhance and expedite your return on those investments, read this book.

Ben Verwaayen
Former CEO of British Telecom and Alcatel-Lucent

PREFACE

Kasper's Employee-generated Learning Journey

I have been involved in e-learning, especially e-learning creation, for over 20 years. My first encounter with e-learning was when I was tasked to build an environment to create and publish learning content and a knowledge base for the Dutch Society for Podiatry. This project evolved from a product I had developed earlier for online help. After delivering the software, they sought my guidance in developing the learning content and knowledge base. I agreed but had limited experience and knowledge in e-learning.

Since I was supposed to be the expert, I started reading about e-learning and asynchronous learning. I discovered instructional design and the world of learning technology. I loved it. It is an exciting mix of technology and learning. Before this project, my work mainly revolved around creating online help systems for software and I often thought my work would become redundant if the software were more user friendly. I discovered that (e-)learning was a much more meaningful occupation for me.

A year later, I joined a learning technology company, the Dutch partner for several learning technology vendors like Blackboard, Questionmark, Moodle, Sakai and Learn eXact. I led the Learning Technology department, while another team focused on producing bespoke e-learning. This team taught me that the predominant method for creating learning content was, and often still is, the ADDIE model.

ADDIE stands for Analysis, Design, Development, Implementation and Evaluation. A colleague explained the process to me. ADDIE consists of five phases. It's a waterfall model, meaning you proceed in sequence from one phase to the next. With this approach, developing a course could span months. We quickly found ourselves in disagreement. My main point was that there was no communication with stakeholders and end users during a large part of the process — a recipe for disaster in my mind. That, combined with the fact that it took months to create a course, put me off completely. I argued that this process was built around the instructional designer rather than the learner. I remember calling it a navel-gazing method. We agreed to disagree as I was convinced there had to be a more effective way to create content.

I was involved in software development early in my career, not as a developer but as a designer. I was part of teams that created a content management system, tools to create online help and my own product for learning content creation. I also co-founded Locatienet, a Dutch web service similar to the later-launched Google Maps. Most of the time, we worked with software development methods that followed waterfall models similar to ADDIE. I knew from these experiences that a process detached from the end users and other stakeholders would only create a little value. Mostly, it would create disappointment.

Meanwhile, working for the learning technology company, I was looking to partner with a simple e-learning authoring tool. One of the tools our company was already partnering with was a very complicated learning content management system. Our customers were requesting a tool that was easier to use. Easygenerator was one of the candidates for that partnership, so I met with the company's product owner and sales representative. Then, between my first and second conversations with them, something happened: my company's CEO decided to leave. He had initially brought me in because he wanted to change the culture and innovate our processes. His decision to leave raised many questions about my role. (Could I achieve the goals without him?) The week my CEO announced his decision, I had my second meeting with Easygenerator. I saw great potential in this company; it was an opportunity to implement my ideas about learning authoring and make them available to a larger group of people. Consequently, I reached out to one of Easygenerator's shareholders. One thing led to another, and just months later, I became the CEO of Easygenerator.

In this capacity, I learned about agile software development for the first time. Instead of a process that takes months to deliver a result, teams of product owners, designers, developers and testers worked in two-week iterations called sprints. A small working piece of software is built, tested and documented in that two-week sprint. At the end of the sprint, the result is shown in a demo to the stakeholders. If they approve the result, it goes live and users can use these small pieces of software immediately. The usage data and the user feedback will tell you how it is received and provide information based on which you can adjust or expand the software if necessary. If it is not approved, the feedback is addressed in the next iteration, or you can even decide to throw out the result and start again. This way of working was an eye-opener for me. I loved the agility of the process and the benefits it brought: an agile approach allows you to stay connected with your stakeholders during development.

If you set out to build a larger feature, it will be divided into smaller chunks, each of which will fit into an iteration. You will build and deliver that feature step by step, iteration after iteration, each producing complete pieces of software. You will start that process with specific goals in mind and sometimes you will discover after a few sprints that you have achieved your goals while not reaching the end of the solution you initially designed. This means you can stop there, you can stop development early. And sometimes you will discover that you are on the wrong track and must start again or make major adjustments to your designs. I loved this flexibility and saw that this agile approach could also apply to e-learning development, providing a potential alternative for ADDIE.

Because of this, I started thinking and writing about implementing these agile methods when creating e-learning: agile e-learning development. It was an overall improvement in the development process and potentially a solution for solving the disconnect between stakeholders and developers during content development.

Easygenerator

When I started working at Easygenerator in December 2010, the company had a sophisticated but complex tool for instructional designers. We had a small user base in the Netherlands and Germany. As the new CEO, I was to build this into a global success.

We were working on improving the tool and tried to open up activities in the US market. Meanwhile, I was still working on the agile e-learning development idea. I started writing articles on the topic for my blog. In 2011, I was asked to become a writer for the blog 'Learning Circuit' by the American Society for Training and Development, the ASTD, now called the ATD. One of my posts on agile e-learning development in the 'Learning Circuit' blog drew a lot of attention and readers. It was even voted into the top 10 valuable blogs of 2011 on elearninglearning.com, an aggregation website. For me, that was an indication that I was on to something meaningful.

But I was not the only one working on improving the e-learning content creation process. Michael Allen created a new methodology called SAM, which he describes in his book *Leaving ADDIE for SAM*.[1] SAM stands for Successive Approximations Model, a model for e-learning design and creation based on agile principles. With it, you get an improvement over ADDIE. SAM uses mock-ups and minor iterations, which help solve the disconnect between end users and stakeholders.

I loved the book and the methodology, and it was a massive improvement over ADDIE solving that disconnect. But meanwhile, I learned that the disconnect was one of many problems with learning content development. Other major issues were the speed and cost of e-learning content development and the inability to keep learning content up to date. It led me to the conclusion that an improved agile e-learning development process with instructional designers wasn't enough to bridge this gap. It needed a more radical change. The solution was to have the business create the learning content. With that, the idea of Employee-generated Learning (EGL) was born.

We were growing and globalizing Easygenerator from a business perspective, but not on the intended scale. So in the spring of 2013, we decided to stop developing and selling our complex instructional design tool. Since that was our only activity, this would mean the company's end. I did get more and more convinced about my EGL idea. Therefore, I pitched it to Easygenerator's shareholders in a meeting. Surprisingly, they gave me the green light.

This decision meant that we had to start from scratch. I decided to stay on and so did our development team. We developed a simple authoring tool with the purpose that anyone would be able to create e-learning without any didactic knowledge, e-learning creation experience, or training. We set out to create a tool that would empower subject matter experts (SMEs) to share their knowledge and experiences and create learning content. A tool that would facilitate EGL. Next to this new focus, we applied all the lessons we had learned from our previous mistakes. This meant that we had to build a genuine software-as-a-service (SaaS) product, that the revenue should be subscription-based and, therefore, 100 per cent recurring. We had to move from selling through a network of partners to direct sales and so on. Nothing stayed the same. We decided to restart in the spring of 2013. Six months later, in October that year, we launched our first version of Easygenerator as an EGL SaaS authoring tool at the DevLearn conference in Las Vegas.

EGL's impact

The initial goal was to improve the creation process of e-learning content. This meant we wanted to solve the disconnect between stakeholders and developers, make e-learning creation faster and cheaper, and make it possible to keep e-learning content up to date. That was successful and the EGL approach is now used by thousands of companies worldwide. In the past ten years, we have learned that EGL could have an even more significant impact than improving the authoring process. We have learned that it is an effective way to scale your development capacity and helps you create small specific courses that otherwise would not have been created. It is a new and effective way to translate and localize content. And when employees start to share their knowledge and experience on a large scale, they create a corporate memory, a corporate brain. This corporate brain contains the knowledge and experiences of the company and it can play an important role in solving two other major issues: knowledge retention and workplace learning.

KNOWLEDGE RETENTION

Employees are constantly leaving their organizations, for various reasons. And each employee who leaves takes with them valuable experience and knowledge. This is a significant loss for the organization. Suppose you capture corporate knowledge and experience in your corporate brain. In that case, you can retain that knowledge and expertise even when employees leave.

WORKPLACE LEARNING

Former Hewlett-Packard CEO Lewis Platt captured the essence of workplace learning in these words: 'If HP knew what HP knows, we'd be three times more productive.'[2]

I love this quote and I believe it to be true. Just think of it. If someone in your organization has a question, someone else may have the answer. If someone encounters a problem, someone else will know the solution to that problem. We would always know what to do if all that information was available. That would make us much more productive. If you have that corporate brain, you have the source that makes achieving this holy grail of workplace learning possible.

Over time, the application and impact of EGL have grown from improving the content authoring process to knowledge retention and workplace or performance support.

This is not a journey I have made just by myself. I started working on the idea of EGL in 2013 and I met Videhi in 2016. I have a more practical approach while she brings loads of theoretical knowledge, which always makes for a great mix. Videhi joined Easygenerator and we've been on this journey together since then.

Videhi's Employee-generated Learning journey

At the beginning of my career, I was tasked with creating help documentation for complex software products. To write this content, I had to dissect every technical detail of the product and use XML-based authoring tools to structure the rigid technical documentation. After a few years, I began to question whether my documentation was helpful for the end users. A quick research showed that while users referred to my work, they didn't find it helpful. This led me to propose creating content in other formats that truly resonated with end users rather than following industry standards.

I moved from the traditional approach to creating help documentation and experimented with making short product videos. I narrated with my Indian accent and applied my raw annotation skills using ancient tools like Zing. This worked – primarily because the content was short, contextual and actionable. I soon realized that I lacked the expertise to create technically accurate videos. So, together with a senior product manager at Cordys R&D (now OpenText), I developed easy methods to let product managers create the videos while I facilitated the process. The quality of the videos was compromised, but the content was relatable and accurate. Product documentation became a secondary source of knowledge. We also built a rich pool of short and catchy product videos created by experts, doubling the end user's trust. Without realizing the impact, we switched from helping users use the product to having SMEs educate them through videos.

The firm's management suggested I work alongside the e-learning team. Still, I found that the team focused solely on using Adobe Captivate and resisted trying anything new. This led me to the fundamental question of how people learn at work and how we can create content that connects with learners in their jobs.

I decided to uncover the truth without following conventional instructional design methods. Those tools only scratched the surface of the broader didactic iceberg. To explore these questions, I experimented with video-based, mobile and blended learning formats, eventually pursuing a Master's in Learning and Technology at the University of Oxford in the UK. I learned about various socio-educational theories, which emphasized the importance of social and situated learning. I began investigating them through a technological lens.

After working with learning and development (L&D) teams in various corporate, think-tank, non-profit and defence organizations around the world, I had a few realizations:

1 What matters most is applying what we learn at work.

2 We learn best from peers and real applications.

3 We learn better through straightforward formats compared to highly interactive click-next courses.

Some of my best learning moments happened on the most challenging projects, facilitating peer-to-peer learning grounded in specific contexts.

In 2016, I met Kasper Spiro. He voiced a passion for democratizing learning and promoting knowledge sharing to create actionable and contextual knowledge by anyone in the organization. (Just like my story of creating product videos!) What resonated the most with me was that his passion was not limited to instructional design tools.

I quickly realized that Kasper spoke of the implementation side. At the same time, I focused on the theoretical side of the same solution, also known as Employee-generated Learning. We have been exploring the EGL approach together, identifying the model's key constructs and discovering product features that are genuinely relevant to the cause. In this book, we discuss the EGL model from theoretical and practical perspectives, providing a comprehensive understanding of how and why L&D professionals can adopt this model.

Notes

1 Allen, M W and Sites, R (2012) *Leaving ADDIE for SAM: An agile model for developing the best learning experiences*, Alexandria, VA: American Society for Training and Development.

2 Sieloff, C G (1999) 'If only HP knew what HP knows': The roots of knowledge management at Hewlett-Packard, *Journal of Knowledge Management*, 3 (1), 47–53. https://doi.org/10.1108/13673279910259385 (archived at https://perma.cc/5CAG-XGZF)

LIST OF ABBREVIATIONS

ADL – advanced distributed learning
AI – artificial intelligence
ADDIE – analysis, design, development, implementation and evaluation
API – application program interface
EGL – Employee-generated Learning
L&D – Learning & Development
LMS – learning management system
LRS – learning record store
LXP – learning experience platform
PSS – performance support systems
ROI – return on investment
R&D – Research & Development
SaaS – Software-as-a-Service
SAM Successive Approximations Model
SCORM – Sharable Content Object Reference Model
SME – subject matter expert
xAPI – experience API

1

What is happening in the world of learning?

Many things impact learning and development (L&D). The Covid-19 pandemic, a changing workforce, new technologies and the ever-increasing speed of business are just a few examples of these changes. Trends such as the skill gap, Big Data, the 70:20:10 model and artificial intelligence (AI) emerge as hypes but eventually settle into a new normal, leaving their mark on the L&D landscape. While many such trends come and go, we've focused on more significant, enduring shifts – the megatrends. (Otherwise, this chapter alone would fill the whole book.) We've distilled them down to four primary, long-term changes that L&D must navigate:

1 From formal to informal learning.
2 From learning to support.
3 From knowledge to skills.
4 From top-down to bottom-up.

All these trends influence each other. That is why we have combined them into one learning diagram (see Figure 1.1). It is an overview of how we look at corporate learning and the changes it is going through. We will first describe these trends in more detail. After that, we will explain our learning diagram and describe how Employee-generated Learning (EGL) fits into that context. This way, we embed EGL in the greater scheme of things.

From formal to informal learning

Formal learning is everything we learn in school, from nursery to university. It also includes all the face-to-face learning, training and e-learning courses we do afterwards. Formal learning can be defined as 'a planned, direct, non-contextual and formulated activity happening off-the-work in a classroom or regulated learning environment'.[1] In other words, it's learning in a specific learning environment (like a classroom) where a teacher determines what you have to learn and you, as a learner, must consume this learning.

Over the past decades, the corporate world has focused primarily on formal learning. First, the focus was on classroom training, often in corporate academies. With the rise of e-learning, this focus shifted to pushing mandatory courses through a learning management system (LMS). This change, however, was cost-driven and not inspired by new didactical insights. E-learning provides a better return on investment (ROI) than classroom training in a physical corporate academy.

Both classroom training and e-learning courses suffer from being detached from the actual working world. As a result, formal learning is well suited for knowledge transfer but less effective for skills development. The prevailing belief is that corporate learning must go beyond mere knowledge sharing, focusing on skills and competency development and adding tangible value to training. To achieve a return on investment, learning efforts must positively impact performance. It's logical, therefore, that other forms of learning, such as informal learning, have emerged.

We define informal learning as all forms of learning that are not top-down organized. It encompasses social learning (learning from peers) and experiential learning (learning by doing). Unlike formal learning, informal learning is unstructured, spontaneous and often unintentional. It frequently happens while someone is solving a problem and includes unplanned learning between individuals as well as learning from experience.

The difference between formal and informal learning is highlighted in the 70:20:10 model created by Robert Eichinger and Michael

Lombardo. They found that competent and experienced workers gain 70 per cent of their knowledge and skills from challenging assignments (learning by doing), 20 per cent from developmental relationships (social learning) and only 10 per cent from coursework and training (formal learning).[2] According to this model, 90 per cent of all learning is informal. Some debate the validity of these numbers because the initial research was a survey of fewer than 200 managers.[3] But it remains clear that formal learning contributes a small percentage to professional development, with informal learning playing a more substantial role.

It wasn't until 2007 when Jay Cross published his book on informal learning that this insight became mainstream and began to impact the L&D space.[4] Together with the 70:20:10 model, it illuminated how L&D professionals had been majorly focusing on formal learning, often sidelining informal and workplace learning. This realization spurred greater attention to informal learning, marking a discernible trend in the industry.

This does not mean that formal learning will disappear. Formal learning is still a well-suited solution for mandatory learning activities like compliance or security training. But these courses are a smaller percentage of a company's learning needs.

It's important to note that switching from a formal to a more informal approach isn't easy for most organizations. Historically, L&D's tools and processes have been geared towards pushing formal learning. These weren't designed with informal learning in mind. To truly embrace informal learning, there's a need for new skills, different processes and alternate tools, a challenge that many L&D departments found daunting.

Under the formal learning model, the L&D department controls what employees learn. They set the pace and timing for learners. In contrast, informal learning isn't about orchestrating but facilitating. Here, the learners take the lead, accessing information when they deem it necessary. It is a very different approach and requires a massive mind-shift from L&D professionals. They have to go from controlling to facilitating; from being in charge towards letting go. Moreover, they need to seamlessly merge these approaches, managing both formal and informal learning. We will discuss this in greater detail in Chapter 3.

The trend is clear. There's a pronounced move from strictly formal learning to a model where informal learning gains prominence.[5] And all aspects of L&D are influenced by this shift.

From learning to support

The goal of corporate learning is transitioning from delivering top-down mandatory courses to enhancing employee efficacy and maintaining their competency. This shift is centred around the learner's needs, not the preferences of the L&D department. Nick Shackleton-Jones, author of *How People Learn*, puts it succinctly: 'Give me Google over an e-learning module any day.'[6] This marks a move away from the traditional 'spoon-fed' approach to providing knowledge accessible within the work context to improve performance. When employees face challenges, they don't want to halt work and sift through an LMS or attend a training session. They seek immediate solutions. But often, Google can't provide company-specific answers.

This highlights the importance of a dedicated database that contains all the company-specific knowledge and experiences to facilitate this workplace learning. Such content can't be generated solely by a central department; it needs to come from the business. This means leveraging a bottom-up approach to curate performance support content. By doing so, you're essentially forming a 'corporate brain' – a reservoir of the organization's collective wisdom. The emerging trend is clear: the focus is shifting from (corporate) learning to (workplace) support. This is, again, a significant shift that requires a fundamental change in how we organize and execute corporate learning. Instead of organizing formal training to help learners acquire knowledge and new skills, we now need to support the worker on the job to help them complete tasks as quickly as possible.

To facilitate this change, you need to either supplement or change your existing learning tools in favour of performance support tools.

This notion is encapsulated in the '5 moments of learning need' model, which we look into in Chapter 4.[7]

The first two trends are closely related. Formal learning stands apart from work – it can't be woven into daily tasks. You have to go to a classroom or learn through an LMS. But informal learning makes it possible to bring learning to the workplace, seamlessly integrating education into the workspace. It allows for simultaneous working and learning. If you look at it from the workplace perspective, bringing learning to the workplace in the form of support requires informal learning approaches.

From knowledge to skills

As knowledge becomes more accessible, finding and retrieving it becomes easier. Because of this, the importance of actually retaining knowledge has become less. Over the last few decades, many of us went from sifting through 20-something volumes of encyclopedias on our parents' bookshelf to a world of information and knowledge readily accessible on our mobile devices. And that is just the beginning. AI will take this to the next level and beyond. Knowing things is less important as long as you're adept at finding reliable information and knowledge and applying that in your work.

Before we delve deeper into these trends, it's crucial to clearly define several terms: skill, competency and being competent. These terms are closely related, but each has a distinct meaning. A skill is something you can do and by nature, skills are generic. Engaging in a conversation in a specific language, using a video conference tool or actively listening during a dialogue are all examples of skills. These abilities are applicable in various contexts, such as any sales role, regardless of the specific organization. To excel as a salesperson within a particular company, mastering these generic skills isn't enough, you must also understand company-specific processes and knowledge. Competencies, such as being familiar with the company's sales call procedures or the pitches for its products or services, are unique to a particular context. When you combine these generic skills with company-specific competencies, you're well on your way to being competent. However, there's another layer: experience and the lessons from failures. Achieving excellence doesn't come solely from training, attending courses or reading books. It requires practical application, occasional failures and the ability to learn from those experiences. In summary, a blend of skills, competencies and experience crafts a competent worker.

Before the 1800s, mastering a trade meant apprenticing under an expert. This hands-on approach was the path to gaining skills, competencies and experience. By learning from the master, you progressed from an apprentice to a competent worker, eventually becoming a master in your own right. This model persists today in traineeships and certain vocational education systems. For instance, one of my (Kasper) sons pursued a career as a chef. His journey involved college one day a week and hands-on training in a restaurant kitchen for the other four days. It was under the guidance of an accomplished chef – a master – that he learned the majority of his craft.

The concept of competency-based training also anchored early corporate learning. It was after the industrial revolution that corporate training truly began to take shape. For instance, in 1872, Hoe and Company sought to enhance their machinists' efficiency. To achieve this, they initiated on-site training. This initiative grew into the first known factory school for workplace learning.[8]

The focus on skills and competencies is something we have lost in most of our educational system because it focuses largely on formal education, and with this it often prioritizes knowledge transfer over practical application. It is the same development that applies to a large part of corporate education. We do know, of course, that learning has real value only when people can apply their knowledge in the workplace; knowledge by itself does not add business value. Knowledge does not help you to do your job better or more efficiently. In corporate education, the trend swings back towards skills development instead of focusing on knowledge transfer. That connects this trend to the first two trends. When you are talking about acquiring skills and competencies, for a large part you have to rely on informal learning that happens while you are working.

This trend in corporate learning emphasizes that we need to make corporate knowledge readily available at our employees' fingertips. Whether it's through a performance support system, an intranet or communication channels like Slack or Yammer, the goal is to have information at the employees' disposal. The aim is to foster informal workplace learning, allowing individuals to hone their skills and competencies through peer interactions and experiential learning. According to Malcolm Gladwell, author of *Blink, Outliers* and many others, it takes 10,000 hours (or approximately 10 years) of deliberate practice to become an expert in something.[9] Cathy Moore, creator of the action mapping method, emphasizes this for corporate learning, putting the focus on the application and behavioural change rather than gaining knowledge.[10]

Corporate learning has long mirrored the traditional education system, emphasizing the transmission of knowledge rather than its practical application. Formal education is typically based on lectures, textbooks and tests that aim to deliver information and build a strong foundation of knowledge. This emphasis on knowledge transfer has also been adopted in corporate training programmes, where the focus is often on teaching theoretical concepts and factual information. This approach is based on the belief that a solid theoretical understanding is needed before practical application can take place. Consequently, corporate training methods have leaned heavily on presentations, e-learning modules and instructor-led sessions. While this ensures a uniform understanding among employees, it often lacks adequate opportunities for practical application or addressing real-world challenges. So the focus is now shifting as people start to value skills above knowledge. Or rather, the focus is shifting *back*. We're reverting to an earlier approach where skills and capabilities took centre stage.

From top-down to bottom-up

The first three trends all lead to a transfer of responsibilities from L&D to the employee. Informal learning, by definition, is something that the employees handle themselves. You can only facilitate this as an organization. Workplace support is also an area where L&D plays a role by putting the information and systems in place, but it's the employee who decides when and how to use it. Also, with the emphasis on skills and competencies, it is largely informal learning that drives this, synonymous with the employee being responsible. All these trends are moving corporate learning from a top-down approach where organizations, through their L&D departments, determine and control employee training, to a bottom-up approach where employees take charge of their development and career path.

L&D plays a pivotal role in meeting the learning needs of an organization. But the effect of the first three trends is a notable shift in L&D's responsibility, moving from an organization-driven approach to one driven by the employees themselves. This shift is the key to the fourth trend: learning is moving from top-down to bottom-up, from controlled to facilitated, from mandatory to democratized learning, from an L&D item to something that is the responsibility of the employee, the worker, the learner.

While L&D once held significant sway over formal learning, the landscape is quickly shifting. Employees are now taking greater charge of their own growth and trajectory. This trend aligns with the changing nature of employment. Nowadays, individuals tend to work for a company for shorter durations. In the US, the average tenure with an employer was about four years as of 2022, a figure that has been on the decline and continues to decrease.[11] Consequently, an employee's professional journey isn't anchored to a single company. They are increasingly at the helm of their own development, often considering what's best for them even if it means looking beyond their current role or company. This shift towards employee-driven goals and aspirations is fuelling the move from top-down to bottom-up learning. Factor in this heightened sense of employee responsibility for development alongside the trends we've discussed and it becomes clear that the top-down, controlling approach adopted by L&D departments is, in large measure, becoming obsolete.

This shift is one of the reasons that learning experience platforms (LXPs) are successful.[12] An LXP is a learning software that, like an LMS, contains learning content. But the content isn't pushed to the learners and doesn't set deadlines for course completion. Here, learners can actively search for training, courses or bite-sized learning resources as they see fit. The emphasis is on a pull rather than push approach. The initiative lies with the employee, the worker, the learner. This gives initiative and control to the learner. The learner determines what to learn and when to learn it. The learner is now in charge. Such a framework signifies a pivot towards a bottom-up approach in corporate learning. However, the ripple effects of this shift transcend merely switching from an LMS to an LXP. It's a move towards democratizing learning on a deeper level, a sentiment central to the philosophy of EGL.

When employees take charge of their own learning and development, it empowers them not only to be self-reliant but also to take on the role of educators for their colleagues. And when a learner becomes a teacher, you get real bottom-up learning – which is the ultimate form of democratization of corporate learning. Employees share their knowledge and experiences with their peers. This is the core notion of EGL: the employee becoming a teacher. EGL is the concretion of this trend from top-down to bottom-up. EGL is the corporate learning creation trend similar to what the creator economy is for social media. SMEs that create content are what influencers are to social media. Josh Bersin, a renowned expert in corporate learning, talent management and HR who founded Bersin & Associates and has authored numerous books in the field, drew an analogy between the creator economy and content creation. He pointed out tools like Easygenerator as creator tools.[13] These tools transform learners into teachers.

The learning diagram

It's clear that these four trends are all interrelated. They enforce each other. And some trends cannot even exist without the others. What's more, together these four trends form the axes of our learning diagram (Figure 1.1), which illustrates our way of looking at the world of corporate learning.

The diagram has four quadrants defined by the beginning and end of the axes. Together they cover the different trends in corporate learning:

- from formal to informal learning (from top left to bottom right)
- from learning to support (from left to right)
- from knowledge to skills (from bottom left to top right)
- and from top-down to bottom-up (from top to bottom)

FIGURE 1.1 The learning diagram

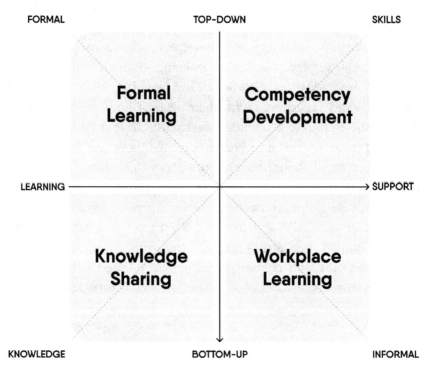

Formal learning: The top-left quadrant is for old-school, top-down formal learning. This refers to learning material that's created by the L&D department or bought from an external vendor, presented as classroom training or an e-learning course.

Competency development: Since the organization owns competencies, this is a top-down-driven quadrant. It is about developing your skills and experiences to fulfil a particular competency. Mainly, learning involves on-the-job coaching or learning through a mentor or a coach. An excellent example of competency development is leadership development.

Knowledge sharing: The bottom-left quadrant is where learning meets bottom-up created learning. This is where SMEs share their knowledge by creating content for their peers. This content can take the form of a course or microlearning. But even if it is a course, these differ significantly from those created by L&D. They tend to be smaller, more practical and aimed at more specific audiences.

Workplace learning: The bottom-right corner represents the essence of workplace learning. It is content created by peers that will help you do your job and solve problems you encounter. If this content is available at your fingertips, it will significantly boost performance.

The four-quadrant diagram is rooted in the trends that are defining the future of corporate learning. It provides context to the foundational shifts taking place within this domain.

Notes

1 Movchan, S (2018) Difference between formal and informal learning [online], Raccoongang.com. Available at: https://raccoongang.com/blog/difference-between-formal-and-informal-learning/ (archived at https://perma.cc/S9N5-3JGN)

2 Lombardo, M M and Eichinger, R W (1996) *The Career Architect Development Planner* (1st ed.), Minneapolis: Lominger. p. iv. ISBN 0-9655712-1-1

3 Harding, R (2022) Debate: The 70:20:10 'rule' in learning and development – the mistake of listening to sirens and how to safely navigate around them, *Public Money & Management*, 42:1, 6–7, DOI: 10.1080/09540962.2021.1951517 (archived at https://perma.cc/E8XR-EMFF)

4 Cross, J (2007) *Informal Learning: Rediscovering the natural pathways that inspire innovation and performance*, San Francisco, CA: Wiley & Sons Publishers

5 Harding, R (2022) Debate: The 70:20:10 'rule' in learning and development – the mistake of listening to sirens and how to safely navigate around them, *Public Money & Management*, 42:1, 6–7, DOI: 10.1080/09540962.2021.1951517 (archived at https://perma.cc/P4NN-A95G)

6 Shackleton-Jones, N (2019) *How People Learn*, London: Kogan Publishers

7 Gottfredson, C and Mosher, B (2010) *Innovative Performance Support: Strategies and practices for learning in the workflow*, Portugal: McGraw-Hill Publishers

8 Learnship (nd) The history (and future) of corporate training, www.learnship.com/en/blog/the-history-and-future-of-corporate-training/ (archived at https://perma.cc/D2QN-KJ39)

9 Gladwell, M (2008) *Outliers: The story of success*, New York: Little, Brown and Co.

10 Moore, C (2017) *Map It: The hands-on guide to strategic training design*, Romania: Montesa Press

11 Bureau of Labor Statistics, Employee Tenure Summary (2022) U.S. Bureau of Labor Statistics, www.bls.gov/news.release/tenure.nr0.htm (archived at https://perma.cc/9G98-XRD9)

12 Santa Maria, A (2021) Closing skill gaps: How a learning experience platform (LXP) makes it happen, https://www.linkedin.com/business/talent/blog/learning-and-development/close-skill-gaps-with-lxp (archived at https://perma.cc/HBC3-U46G)

13 Bersin, J (2022) The creator market for corporate learning: A massive, still untapped market, The Joshbersin Company, joshbersin.com/wp-content/uploads/2022/04/L_D-04_22-The-Creator-Market-for-Corporate-Learning-Report-v2.pdf (archived at https://perma.cc/JN8R-5PRY)

2

Broadcasters, streamers and creators

We believe that the *top-down to bottom-up* trend led to the most fundamental changes in corporate learning. It also had the most significant impact on the idea of Employee-generated Learning. But interestingly, this trend doesn't only apply to corporate learning. Its impact on music, broadcasting, hospitality and travel is slowly but fundamentally changing the thread of our society.

The film, television and media industry

Not so far in the past, television was the supreme medium. With it, broadcasting companies dictated the content and timing: the news began at eight, followed by a soap opera, and finally, a game show at night. Viewers had minimal control, limited to changing the channel or turning off the TV altogether. This was a purely top-down approach, with broadcasters pushing programmes to the audience and holding all the control. Over time, the growing desire for autonomy began to influence viewer behaviour and preferences. They wanted to choose what to watch and when.

I (Kasper) saw this evolution firsthand. Born in 1962, I initially experienced black-and-white TV. In the Netherlands. We had just two channels with limited broadcasting hours. When I had to choose between playing outside or watching television, playing outside almost always won.

> It wasn't until 1989 that commercial broadcasting began in the Netherlands. By 2000, we had MTV, a channel devoted to music 24/7, in contrast to the mere 30 minutes dedicated to the Dutch Top 40 that we had before. As more channels surfaced, viewers found themselves with an array of choices.
>
> The rise of videotapes in the late seventies was transformative. For the next two decades, the allure of video tapes – and the video rental business they spawned – was that they provided choice. Viewers no longer had to rely solely on broadcasters; they could rent a movie and watch it whenever they liked. By the early 2000s, digital video recorders (DVRs) started to gain traction.
>
> I was an early adopter of TiVo, the first device I knew that allowed you to record from TV to a hard disk. The best thing was that you could set your TiVo to always record your favourite series' episodes or anything you saw on the TV guide. This way, you could build your own library of things to watch whenever you wanted. It was the first time that I felt a sense of control over my viewing experience.

In 1998, Hong Kong Telecom launched iTV, the first video-on-demand service. It allowed you to watch a video without leaving your home to get it. These early video-on-demand services later developed into streaming providers like Netflix, which started as a mail-order subscription service that would deliver DVDs to your home.

The rise of on-demand services changed the world of television forever. Previously, television was a broadcasting-based model, pushing programmes to viewers based on a predetermined schedule. Streaming services, however, ushered in an era where viewers could pull their desired content, choosing what to watch, when and on their preferred device. This transition marked a significant shift from top-down broadcasting to a more bottom-up approach.

Yet the transformation of media consumption didn't stop with streaming. The emergence of social media platforms like CompuServe set the stage, but the game-changers were platforms like MySpace in 2003, Facebook in 2004, YouTube in 2005 and Twitter in 2006. Social media was born.[1] While initially designed for communication,

FIGURE 2.1 Broadcaster, streamer and creator platforms

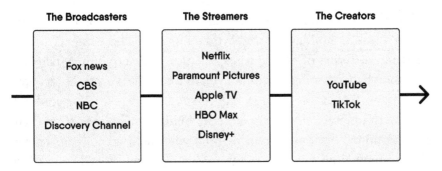

these platforms quickly morphed into hubs for user-generated content. Social media became a platform to create and publish your own content. The number of apps is staggering. The list of social media sites is huge and most of them are focused on creating and sharing content:

- LinkedIn (2003)
- MySpace (2003)
- Facebook (2004)
- YouTube (2005)
- Twitter (2006)
- Pinterest (2010)
- Instagram (2010)
- TikTok (2016)

What distinguishes social media from traditional broadcasting or even streaming services is its dual function: it's a platform both for consuming and for creating content. Consider YouTube: not only can you watch videos, you can also create and upload your own, transitioning from a passive viewer to an active creator. Platforms such as LinkedIn, Pinterest, Instagram and TikTok followed suit, emphasizing user-generated content. The progression from traditional broadcasting to on-demand streaming and now to personal content creation (see Figure 2.1) represents a profound change in how we engage with media.

The hospitality industry

Before the rise of the web and the existence of apps, people predominantly booked holidays through travel agents. These agents had a particular offering of hotels, transportation and activities. Much like television broadcasting schedules, you had a range of options (accommodations, flights, car rentals), but the selection was set. You couldn't add anything yourself. You could only build your holiday from their predetermined options, mirroring how you might create your television evening from the set programmes being broadcast. These travel agents, then, were much like the *broadcasters* of the hospitality industry.

But with the surge of the internet and the emergence of platforms, the game changed. Services like Booking.com, Skyscanner, Expedia and Agoda made it possible for travellers to assemble bespoke holidays, parallel to streaming on-demand from services like Netflix. These platforms, in essence, played the role of streaming services, transferring control to the user. These services did to the travel industry what Netflix did for television: they put the user in charge. Now travellers could choose where to stay, how to get there and what to do, unrestricted by the limitations of a packaged deal. These hospitality apps are, in fact, the *streamers* of the hospitality industry.

Much as in the world of film and television, the evolution in the travel sector continues. Just as TikTok and YouTube transformed viewers into content creators, platforms like Airbnb and CouchSurfing have empowered travellers to take on the role of hosts. They're the *creators* of the hospitality industry. You're no longer just a consumer, you can craft your own unique hospitality experience and share it globally. This parallels the shift in television: moving from broadcasters, to streamers and ultimately to individual creators.

Broadcasters, streamers and creators

The development of content delivery and creation is evident across various sectors. In the news industry, broadcasters took many shapes and forms, from medieval minstrels to print media, radio and televised news. This top-down broadcasting model was followed by streamers: platforms like CNN and the Huffington Post offered a more on-demand selection, allowing consumers to access news as per their convenience. The advent of platforms like Reddit and Twitter took this a step further. Not only can you consume news, you can also participate in its creation and dissemination, embracing the role of a citizen journalist. This movement shows the shift from a top-down to a bottom-up approach. In all these examples, we see the change from broadcasters to streamers to creators. Let's reiterate the meaning of these terms:

- **Broadcasters:** Organizations that push content to the consumer in a take-it-or-leave-it manner. You can either consume it or turn away from it; you cannot change or influence the content.
- **Streamers:** You still can't change the content but you have a much more comprehensive selection of content to choose from. The critical thing is that *you* select the content. Streaming services put the consumer of the content in charge.
- **Creators:** Here, not only do you have the autonomy to select and consume, but platforms empower you to wear the creator's hat. You can produce content and circulate it amongst a broader audience.

With this process, we witness the democratization of content creation in our society. The monopoly on content creation held by large organizations is broken. Now, anyone and everyone can step into the limelight as a content creator.

Broadcasters, streamers and creators applied to corporate learning

The switch from broadcasting to streaming and finally to creating is also seen in corporate learning (see Figure 2.2). In the days before Jay Cross, the 70:20:10 model and informal learning, L&D teams had

FIGURE 2.2 Broadcaster, streamer and creator platforms in corporate learning

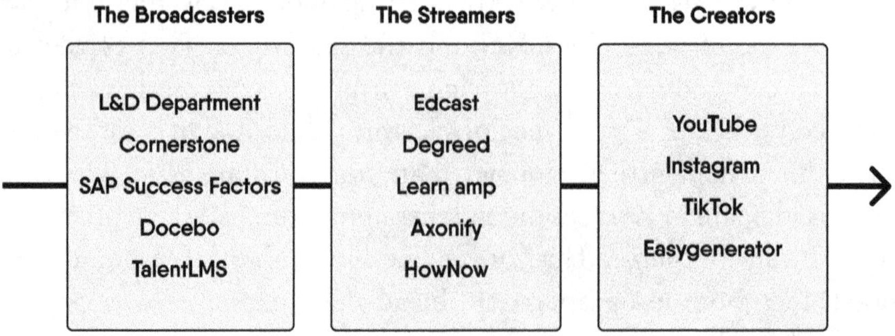

The Broadcasters	The Streamers	The Creators
L&D Department Cornerstone SAP Success Factors Docebo TalentLMS	Edcast Degreed Learn amp Axonify HowNow	YouTube Instagram TikTok Easygenerator

near-total control. Their domain, largely rooted in formal learning, was characterized by the creation and scheduling of face-to-face training or e-learning courses. They created and planned face-to-face learning or e-learning courses and pushed those to the learners via LMSs. Such a top-down approach likened the L&D teams to broadcasters, with LMSs playing the role of their broadcasting tools. But as with television, people wanted to take matters into their own hands: employees wanted to be in charge of their development. We described this in Chapter 1 when introducing the trends. As people move towards spending shorter durations with a single employer, the motivation to take charge of their own development gets amplified.

> I (Kasper) started working at 22 years old; I'm now 61. Over my 39-year career, I've worked for eight different companies, averaging just under five years at each. For me, taking my personal development into my own hands made sense. In my first job, where I worked from 1985 to 1990, I teached computer-based bookkeeping to unemployed people. In my second job, I was an information designer. I designed custom-made knowledge management and performance support solutions. Only by taking responsibility for my own development was I able to transform from a teacher into an information designer. My first employer would have had no benefits from training me in that direction. It had to be me. I continued on that road of self-development, becoming a manager, a CEO and a business owner.

What's more, many people now work in jobs that didn't even exist when they were getting their formal education. My role as CEO of an SaaS company is an excellent example of that. I started working in 1985. The World Wide Web launched in April 1993. In my student days, SaaS companies didn't exist yet and neither did the web. All these things emerged when I had already been progressing in my professional career for some time, which is why most of the knowledge I use in my job I learned *after* finishing my formal education. Because of the emergence of all these new jobs and roles, people must take their personal development into their own hands, continuing it after finishing their formal education. This is the driver behind lifelong learning.

To keep up with the world's constant state of change, to progress in your career or simply to perform your job function, you need to be in a continual learning and development state. This learning falls on the individual, not the organization. Learning that arises out of a work scenario is inherently learner-driven, embodying the essence of bottom-up learning. The most an L&D department can do in this evolving landscape is to ensure that the right tools and mechanisms are available to deliver pertinent learning content right where it's needed: at the workplace.

Turning colleagues into creators

Learners being responsible for their own learning is not the end of the story. Social media platforms like YouTube and TikTok, the most extensive creator platforms in the world, are also the largest learning platforms. This is also relevant to corporate learning. These platforms not only enable content consumption, they also empower individuals to become creators themselves. The parallels between social media and corporate learning are evident.

Now more than ever, companies are constantly learning and adapting to maintain a competitive edge. Traditional L&D departments often find it challenging to keep pace with the swift changes in business, given the specific and dynamic business knowledge needed to generate timely and relevant learning content. This gap creates an opening for employees to play a pivotal role. With their operational knowledge and insights, employees can share vital information more rapidly and effectively than traditional L&D methods would allow.

By embracing their role as creators and teachers, learners within the corporate setting capture and share their niche knowledge and experience, using user-friendly content creation platforms. This emerging trend of employee-generated content has proven to be a driving force behind successful knowledge sharing within organizations. And as we saw earlier in this chapter, it is a general trend towards the democratization of content creation and with that, this has become an unstoppable change.

The following chapters will provide further information on the theories underpinning EGL. However, while EGL might seem to stem from informal, bottom-up, skill-enhancing content, its true foundation is in situated and social learning. These have always guided how workers learn from each other within authentic job environments, where the goal is to apply oneself to learn and perform on the job.

Note

1   Ortiz-Ospina, E (2019) The rise of social media. Published online at OurWorldInData.org. Retrieved from: ourworldindata.org/rise-of-social-media (archived at https://perma.cc/39JK-9HYC) [Online Resource]

3

Introduction to Employee-generated Learning (EGL)

The need for EGL

Employee-generated Learning is a fundamental shift in how we deal with learning and learning content creation in a corporate environment. Before starting to define and explain what EGL is, we'll first address *why* there's a need for this fundamental change. What were the root causes that led to us developing this approach?

Currently, e-learning creation is predominantly done through the ADDIE method, a five-staged instructional design framework used for creating training content. (If you haven't read the preface, ADDIE stands for analysis, design, development, implementation and evaluation.) It's a waterfall method, which means that you have to finish a phase before starting the next one. ADDIE has its fair share of disadvantages, but the most significant one is that it makes learning content development slow and expensive. We illustrate the traditional process of e-learning development with ADDIE in Figure 3.1.

The ADDIE model requires that training materials be crafted by either in-house instructional designers in L&D or external agencies. Initially, these designers, whether inside the organization or from outside, consult internal subject matter experts (SMEs) to shape the training content. Once crafted, the content is uploaded onto an LMS for learners to access.

FIGURE 3.1 The traditional process of e-learning content development with ADDIE

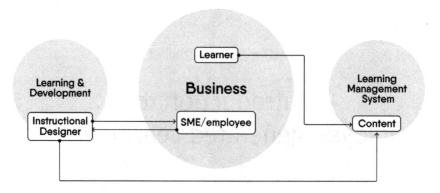

But there are inherent problems with this model. We've already identified the disconnect between stakeholders and e-learning developers
as one primary concern. A closer look at the development process
reveals another major shortcoming. In this conventional model, the
instructional designer, often distant from the daily workings of the
business, is tasked with creating the e-learning content. Since they
lack first-hand knowledge of business-specific issues, they need to
extract this knowledge through interviews with SMEs who *do* have
this knowledge. Turning all that insight into digestible e-learning
content involves deciphering conflicting inputs, verifying the collected
data and more, prolonging the development process. This is the main
reason that e-learning content development is so slow. And because
time is money, it's also why creating e-learning content is so expensive. Research shows that creating one hour of e-learning takes
between 90 and 240 hours of work.[1] Plus, that process can cost
between $10,000 and $30,000.[2]

So the key problem with creating e-learning content is that the
instructional designer is responsible for creating and maintaining the
learning material despite lacking business knowledge. On top of that,
instructional designers focus on content creation; maintenance isn't a
main concern. And even if they would pay attention to maintenance,
they're not connected to the business. They don't keep up with industry news, procedural changes or up-to-date best practices. The
instructional designer is, therefore, incapable of updating any learning

material. The course stays the same. So, learning content becomes outdated in weeks – or worse, even days. And because of prolonged production times, in some cases e-learning courses even become outdated by their publishing date.

Most e-learning courses in a given LMS are outdated. In my (Kasper) previous job, I implemented Moodle, an LMS, for a large oil company. After creating the new learning environment, we got to the last stage: migrating courses from the company's old LMS into Moodle. They had thousands of courses. I asked if they were sure the courses were all up to date and they affirmed that they should be. Nevertheless, I asked them to do a quick check. We selected 100 courses at random and got SMEs to verify their relevance. The result was shocking. Not one course was completely up to date. Some of the courses were two years old, but even those published three weeks previously contained outdated information. Later, I discovered that the problem with maintaining content was not isolated to just this oil company: it is a widespread issue. It led me to a sad conclusion about e-learning content: **companies spend a lot of time and money to teach people outdated stuff**.

On top of the issues with speed, cost and maintenance, there is another development we need to take into account. Corporate organizations undergo fundamental changes; with that, the nature of the learning content also changes. There is significantly more specialization within companies than two decades ago and this triggers the need for specific learning content aimed at smaller groups of people.

As per a report by Josh Bersin, nearly 70 per cent of learning content is developed within organizations.[3] This trend persists despite the presence of prominent content vendors such as Udemy, LinkedIn Learning, Skillsoft, Coursera and many others. This internal content development is likely attributed to the unique processes, products, safety procedures, internal strategies and compliance rules that vary from one company to another. Each organization has its distinct requirements that call for tailored learning materials.

Our customers at Easygenerator report a substantial increase in specific learning requests for smaller groups. On top of this, companies have multiple divisions, often spread out over many different countries. Learning content often needs to be adjusted for each division and the same goes for countries. When creating learning content, you need to consider language, legislation and culture. This means that an e-learning course not only has to be translated, it has to be localized. It must be altered to fit a specific area or country's culture, rules and regulations. All these things lead to the need for specific courses aimed at smaller groups, significantly complicating content creation and maintenance. Not to mention, having an instructional designer to create courses for these smaller audiences is too expensive.

The EGL approach

EGL encompasses all the learning and performance materials that are *not* crafted by e-learning specialists. With an EGL approach, the *employees* are in charge of creating and maintaining learning content. That is why it's called Employee-generated Learning. Any employee has the potential to step into the role of a course author. These are people from the business, the SMEs.

Shifting to an EGL approach addresses all the problems linked to traditional L&D methods. The content creation process with EGL is illustrated in Figure 3.2.

The SMEs, not the instructional designers, create and maintain the learning content, but this doesn't mean that the latter no longer play a role in content creation. They can still initiate, coach, guide and co-author as long as they don't solely take over the responsibility of creating and maintaining the content. The SME who creates the courses is also the person who makes sure they are kept up to date (something that should be relatively easy for them). Whenever a course author notices a change in day-to-day operations, they should update the course.

FIGURE 3.2 The process of content development with EGL

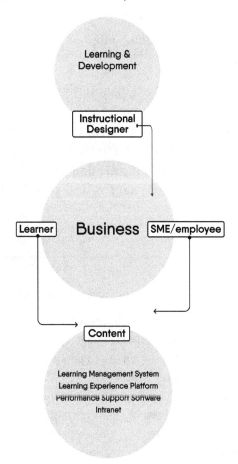

Here are a few real-life applications of EGL in action, shared by some of our customers:

- Product managers who create user training and documentation for their products.
- A founder and CEO creating content about the company's values and culture.
- A specialist informing co-workers about trends and changes they will have on products, competitors, methods and specialized topics of interest.

- An SME who creates an addendum course with the company's specifics for a default methodology.
- SMEs creating content around internal processes, best practices and how-tos.

The easiest way for someone to identify the topics for EGL is aptly put by Louise Puddifoot, L&D expert and founder of scale-up people development company Willow & Puddifoot: 'There's that niche part to every role that is only applicable to the project or team or organization that you are in at the moment, and you need someone that can put the information in the context of the specific situation of the organization.'[4]

CASE STUDY
Extra development capacity for specific pieces of content

A global data measurement firm with multiple divisions could not meet its diverse training needs. The ratio of L&D resources to training requests was unmanageable. So, the central L&D team had to prioritize strategic training projects and had no time for smaller requests.

Recognizing this gap, the L&D unit adopted an EGL approach, entrusting individual departments with the responsibility of creating their training content. The L&D team provided other teams with easy-to-use tools and created an internal site with general guidelines for creating effective training material.

Now the firm has over 1,000 employees who actively create content through a system of peer-to-peer knowledge sharing. This shift has not only alleviated the L&D team's workload but has also empowered it to provide solutions to those with niche requirements. All the while, the core L&D team maintains its focus on overarching strategic projects.

The applicability of EGL

EGL is not a solution for everything. So where does it have the biggest impact? EGL is most potent with *company-specific* learning and

TABLE 3.1 L&D-generated vs EGL content

	L&D-generated	Employee-generated
Target audience size	Impacts more than 12.5% of your workforce	Impacts less than 12.5% of your workforce
Target audience geography	Global	Regional, local or specific projects
Priority for L&D	Top 10	Not top 10
Stakeholder level	Senior leadership	Directors and below
Topic type	Generic content like security and compliance	Business-specific topics
Speed of change	Low	High

performance content. Content that describes business processes and applications that change frequently. Bottom-up content. Table 3.1 shows a broader overview of the criteria determining whether the content suits an EGL approach.

There is also a more theoretically driven way to distinguish EGL content from non-EGL content. Let's look at Figure 3.3. This illustrates Bloom's Taxonomy, which divides the creation of learning into six levels, ranging from very simple (remembering) to complex forms of learning (creating).[5]

We found that EGL is the most effective in the first three levels of learning Bloom's Taxonomy: *remembering*, *understanding* and *applying*. We also found that EGL content must be applicable to add business value. So, EGL is the most powerful in the first three levels and should always cover the third level: applying. This doesn't mean that employees can't write content or be responsible for maintenance for the higher levels. But in those cases, the instructional designer should be much more involved in making sure that the proper didactics are implemented to reach those higher levels of learning.

Formal learning is, by definition, top-down driven. It consists of content created by the learning department and delivered to the learner. However, there is a shift taking place. While the content for talent development is often generic, such as theories on certain management philosophies, a significant portion of formal learning is

FIGURE 3.3 The division of content creation between instructional designers and SMEs based on Bloom's Taxonomy

Level	Question	Verbs	Role
Creating	Can the learner create new product or point of view?	Assemble, construct, create, design, develop, formulate, write	Instructional designer
Evaluating	Can the learner justify a stand or decision?	Appraise, argue, defend, judge, select, support, value, evaluate	
Analysing	Can the learner distinguish between different parts?	Appraise, compare, contrast, criticize, differentiate, discriminate, distinguish, examine, experiment, question, test	
Applying	Can the learner use information in a new way?	Choose, demonstrate, dramatize, employ, illustrate, interpret, operate, schedule, sketch, solve, use, write	Subject matter experts
Understanding	Can the learner explain ideas or concepts?	Classify, describe, discuss, explain, identify, locate, recognize, report, select, translate, paraphrase	
Remembering	Can the learner recall or remember the information?	Define, duplicate, list, memorize, recall, repeat, state	

directly related to business needs. This includes courses on compliance or security, which can be more generic. Such content is primarily crafted by instructional designers or third parties. Due to the stability of these topics, these training programmes don't require frequent updates, making maintenance relatively straightforward.

It's important to understand that even with L&D-generated formal training, the role of the SME is still significant. You're likely to employ a top-down approach in this context, with L&D leading the course design. However, we believe the relevant SME should be responsible for authoring and updating the content. Given their profound understanding of the law and its application, entrusting them with this task ensures a quicker, more cost-effective and easily maintainable process.

Once, I (Kasper) met with a customer from an asset management company. During the meeting with their L&D team, which spearheaded their EGL initiative, they introduced me to their primary Easygenerator users. Surprisingly, both were from the compliance department, with neither having a background in learning or education. If memory serves, one was a financial specialist and the other a lawyer. However, it was these two who took charge of all compliance training and certifications, with the support of the learning department.

Specific formal learning programmes address work processes, the use of supporting tools and software, updates on changes and other business-related subjects. These subjects tend to evolve rapidly. As a result, they are often developed by SMEs. This is because entrusting business professionals with the creation and maintenance of these courses ensures they remain current. While there's an increasing role for SMEs in this area, control over such content largely remains with the L&D department. When implementing what we refer to as the regulated approach to EGL, organizations can enjoy the benefits of EGL – efficiency, cost-effectiveness and easy maintenance – without requiring expertise in the tool or instructional design background. We delve deeper into regulated EGL in Chapter 6.

The impact of EGL

Developing learning content directly with SMEs is substantially faster and cheaper than developing learning content through a central learning department. This approach not only expedites content creation, it also meets the rising demand for tailored training. It is also a faster and cheaper solution for translating and localizing content. And by entrusting local employees, you ensure the content is culturally relevant and accurate as they possess the unique insights necessary for such tasks. Perhaps most importantly, an EGL approach is the only way to keep your content up to date. Let's look deeper into the impacts of EGL.

Speed of creation and maintenance

SMEs possess extensive job expertise and understand the required knowledge and skills more accurately than L&D people. Moreover, they encounter the questions and problems related to their jobs. So enabling them to ensure that these common queries are adequately addressed will build a rich knowledge pool. With EGL, SMEs can take the initiative instead of waiting for L&D to develop content. They can cater to many learning needs among themselves.

Considering the dynamic nature of knowledge and skills, SMEs are in the best position to assess and promptly update relevant content pieces. Unlike L&D, which may have to undergo the entire cycle for minor updates, SMEs can efficiently make adjustments. This streamlined content maintenance process benefits both L&D and the business units, making it significantly easier to keep the content up to date.

One of our customers, a large telco company, reported that with content creation through EGL, they reduced time to market by 90 per cent. In other words, creating and distributing learning content was 10 times faster. They now create five times more training resources than before implementing EGL, using 75 per cent fewer L&D resources.

Increased L&D capacity at lower costs

It is a reality that L&D departments cannot fulfil every learning request, so by empowering SMEs to create and maintain content you're effectively embedding a quasi-L&D professional in every team. This approach allows L&D to increase its capacity, as numerous learning needs are now fulfilled within the internal business units. As a result, the capacity of L&D increases exponentially since a majority of learning needs are directly addressed within business units. The department can operate on a leaner budget, reallocating resources towards pivotal, high-level activities. Also, there's no longer a need to contract external agencies or purchase expensive interactive tools.

Furthermore, EGL allows employees to take control of tactical knowledge. With EGL, training capacity isn't determined by the size of the L&D team but by the amount of participation from the business in the EGL initiative. This also allows you to create niche content that otherwise would be sidelined because of a lack of capacity or knowledge. Very specific courses for small groups of learners are an example of that. Localized courses for each region or country are another. With EGL, a whole category of content is unlocked. Content that previously could not be created because L&D just did not have the knowledge for it.

Because of EGL, L&D can address the growing number of small to medium learning requests by enabling employees to self-serve their needs with EGL. As a result, the core L&D team can focus exclusively on global strategic endeavours. They can focus on strategic management rather than catering to the needs of small groups. This renders L&D more creative and productive.

CASE STUDY

EGL as a response to L&D budget cuts

A few years ago, a large telecom company in the Netherlands had its L&D budget cut by 7 per cent. Among other things, the 14-person learning staff was down to just four. Meanwhile, they had growing backlogs because of the increasing demand for learning content.

They implemented an EGL approach. The responsibility for fulfilling training requests shifted from the L&D department to the business units. L&D became responsible only for quality assurance and guidance, not for content creation.

Now, their time to market for learning content development is 12 times shorter. This means that employees create e-learning courses 12 times faster than instructional designers did. They also report that they now have a five times higher output than before, with only 25 per cent of their previous resources.

Increased employee productivity

On a typical workday, an employee spends around 20 per cent of their time just searching and gathering needed information, as per a 2012 McKinsey report.[6] Using recorded knowledge can cut down on this time and prevent the repetition of past mistakes. EGL focuses on this exact idea: capturing and sharing essential content.

When an organization has a pool of knowledge collected over a period from its entire workforce, it can operate at an enormous advantage. Mistakes don't have to happen again, effective solutions can be put into action swiftly and decisions can be made promptly and correctly.

A large academic hospital in the Netherlands has embraced an EGL approach, with nurses and doctors regularly producing e-learning courses for their colleagues. Medical institutions rely heavily on instruction of junior staff by more senior colleagues; additionally, turnover is typically very high. These EGL courses quickly became popular and effective because they train less experienced staff on situations they might not have encountered yet. Learners trust the material because it's coming straight from their peers. Courses cover topics like pain management for different patient demographics and the utilization of various medical equipment. This content boosts the efficiency of knowledge transfer, thereby improving overall organizational productivity.

Bridging the skills gap of employees

EGL also addresses the skills gap. The skills gap is the difference between the skills an employer requires and the skills the workforce, or an individual employee, possesses. Maintaining an up-to-date skill set requires ongoing learning throughout one's career. While formal training is one method, much of this skill acquisition happens on the job. L&D can organize the formal training, but on-the-job learning is primarily facilitated by L&D with EGL acting as the driving force.

At a data analytics and consulting firm, a manager recognized that his team had unique skill requirements based on their specific projects and clients. The formal L&D programmes didn't cater to these distinct needs. To address this, the manager began compiling existing training resources like Word documents and PowerPoint presentations to establish a specialized academy for a major client project.

As the firm's needs evolved, they incorporated our EGL authoring solution, enhancing their makeshift academy into a comprehensive corporate learning hub tailored to that specific project. What's more, they even shared some courses with the client, allowing both parties to benefit. This approach was a hit, inspiring other teams to create tailored academies for their projects and clients.

Remarkably, this entire EGL-driven transformation occurred without any intervention from the L&D department or any specialized learning experts.

Creating a corporate brain

We initially designed EGL as a way to address the slow pace, high cost and upkeep challenges associated with creating learning content. However, we soon realized its potential reached far beyond that.

When employees leave a company, they take with them invaluable skills, experiences and knowledge. This is especially true for specialized employees who've accumulated years of expertise. Their departure means the organization loses not only their foundational knowledge but also insights gleaned over years through routine tasks, unique problem solving and on-the-job learning. The way to combat this is by capturing all this knowledge in a corporate brain.

By fostering a culture of knowledge sharing, with the help of EGL, SMEs can document their unique corporate insights. This knowledge repository, or corporate brain, acts as the organization's central hub for intelligence. It houses technical know-how, practical insights, best practices, basic skills, frequently asked questions, specialized expertise and intricate company-specific procedures. It's not just about creating formal courses but capturing operational and tactical content that assists in problem solving, decision making and continuous growth.

The corporate brain isn't just a tool for performance support or workplace learning, it's a solution to a pressing problem many companies face: the knowledge loss that comes with growing rates of employee turnover. And why is this a pressing problem? Because there's a noticeable trend that today's employees tend to stay with a single employer for shorter durations compared with past decades.[7] Additionally, this trend has been enforced by the Great Resignation, a during- and post-Covid mass resignation of employees across several industries.[8] To top things off, the Baby Boom generation began to retire, followed by Generation X.[9] These two generations form a substantial part of our current workforce and they hold an immense amount of knowledge and experience – knowledge that needs to be captured soon.

A large aeroplane manufacturing company faced this exact problem due to its high age demographic. A significant portion of its workforce was approaching retirement age. This was especially concerning because these employees held specialized knowledge about everything from plane design and manufacturing to sales and maintenance, which was unique to the company. Such information couldn't just be acquired from the outside; it had been accumulated and refined internally over years.

If the senior employees retired without passing it on, the company would lose vital information, endangering its core operations and even its future. In response to this looming crisis, the company took several strategic steps:

- It began a rigorous process of capturing all its procedures and workflows in a knowledge management system.

- It hired replacements two years before an employee's scheduled retirement to ensure there was ample time for a direct and comprehensive knowledge transfer.

- Newly hired employees were paired with their retiring counterparts. This mentor–mentee setup allowed for an in-depth, hands-on learning experience, ensuring no detail, however minute, was missed.

- New recruits were responsible for consistently updating the knowledge management system with their learnings.

Had the company adopted a knowledge-sharing culture from the start, this crisis would have been avoided altogether. Moving forward, the company is attentively nurturing this culture to safeguard its corporate brain.

Employee retention

EGL empowers employees to take control of their learning and development, allowing them to share their skills, knowledge and expertise with their co-workers. As a direct result, EGL instils a palpable sense of recognition and appreciation within employees. This feeling of being valued not only amplifies their satisfaction but also plays a pivotal role in increasing retention rates within the organization.

While learners undoubtedly gain from this system, the creators – the authors and the knowledge sharers – derive immense satisfaction too. The act of sharing knowledge offers them a platform to showcase their expertise, making them feel more appreciated. Furthermore, the process of documenting and sharing their knowledge provides them with unique learning opportunities. This contributes to a higher sense of happiness and job satisfaction, which invariably leads to improved retention rates.

Feedback from our customers reinforces the efficacy of EGL. A recurring theme is the trust placed in learning content crafted by peers. This content, created from the first-hand experience of peers, often outshines material developed externally or by L&D departments, in terms of both ratings and results.

CASE STUDY
Moving content creation in-house

An Austrian jet operator firm faced challenges with pilot training, leading to high job dissatisfaction and attrition rates. They initially bought expensive off-the-shelf courses, which were not tailored to the firm's specific requirements and were difficult to track. They had to purchase additional content in order to update the policies, which caused further delays of up to a month or more. But the content was generic and didn't meet pilots' specific needs, which wasted their limited time. The firm needed a solution to deliver training faster, save costs and provide highly relevant information to maximize pilot satisfaction and retention.

The firm decided to get content creation done in-house. They chose a simple authoring and distribution setup, including Easygenerator, to implement EGL. L&D now had complete control over the process and was assured of tailored and up-to-date training content. They reduced the time needed to release new training from up to a month to less than a day. Pilots received timely and focused training on policies and procedures. The firm saved time and money while experiencing an increase in retention rate of over 20 per cent. Employees appreciated the tailored content, resulting in positive feedback and satisfaction.

Learning at the speed of business

In today's fast-moving business world, it's essential to keep learning at the same pace as the business is growing. Organizations need to make sure their employees' knowledge and skills are always up to date. This 'living content' means that learning materials need to be created and updated quickly. But traditional L&D methods sometimes struggle to keep up with this fast-paced knowledge growth. The most sensible way to solve this problem is by putting the employee in charge of knowledge creation and maintenance. Their tactical knowledge can be used in the workplace to produce concrete results. EGL enables the sharing and constant updating of this knowledge, ensuring it stays relevant and helpful for everyone.

In some companies, at first glance EGL might seem unnecessary, especially if certain parts of the business have longstanding, established processes. But even in such settings, different departments can still benefit immensely from an EGL approach.

Take, for example, a global consumer goods company. While their factories represent a steady and unchanged aspect of their business, departments like sales, legal, HR and product development experience rapid shifts. The learning department found it challenging to produce timely training materials, especially for new products. So, the company pivoted. They integrated EGL into the product development process, giving teams the tools and autonomy to create their own learning materials. This ensured that as soon as a new product was developed, it was immediately paired with the required training.

This EGL strategy, starting in product development, has since spread across the company, with over 2,000 experts from various departments now actively creating and updating content. This evolution showcases the importance and versatility of EGL, even in businesses with a mix of slow-moving and fast-paced departments.

Moving from face-to-face training to e-learning

Blended learning is often defined as a mix of face-to-face and online learning. We define it a bit differently. For us, the key element defining a learning type lies not in the medium but in the timing: whether participants learn all at once (synchronous learning) or at their own rhythm (asynchronous learning). Blended learning is a mix of the two.

There are many models of blended learning: the face-to-face driver model, the rotation model, the flex model, the list goes on. But the one that is often used in combination with EGL is the 'flipped classroom'. This model dates back to the nineties when two chemistry teachers, Jonathan Bergmann and Aaron Sams, noticed that many of their students were struggling with their homework assignments. As with most secondary school classes, they taught in class and gave homework on the subjects discussed during the lesson. But it wasn't working. This led them to reverse the learning process: recording lectures for students to watch before class and using class time for assignments. This way, whenever a student got stuck, the teachers were there to help and explain. This approach resulted in several benefits. Students could repeatedly view lectures at their convenience and arrived in class prepared with knowledge and questions. The students were much more engaged and the learning outcomes were better. In class, the students focused on applying their newfound knowledge – not just acquiring it. Jonathan and Aaron coined the term *flipped classroom* and in 2021 they co-authored *Flip Your Classroom: Reach every student in every class every day*, which hugely popularized this form of blended learning.[10]

So, how does EGL relate to the flipped classroom? It turns out that in corporate training programmes, the flipped classroom combined with EGL brings forth distinct benefits. Instead of a recorded lecture, there's an employee-generated e-learning course. Learners take these courses as preparation for the synchronous session, the face-to-face training. There, they apply the learnings they gained from e-learning through discussions, simulations and role-play activities.

CASE STUDY

Blended learning for global, scalable training

A prominent home appliances company in Europe faced training challenges in ensuring their products, sold through a partner network, were well represented by local sales agents. Their initial training strategy was three-fold:

1 They conducted three-day onsite training sessions across more than 30 countries, each in its native language.

2 A specialized team of trainers were travelling to all these locations.

3 They supplemented these training sessions with third-party e-learning courses.

This approach was both costly and lacked scalability. To pivot, the company integrated an LMS and an authoring tool for SMEs. With the L&D department's assistance, small trainer groups began converting the standard training content into e-learning modules, focusing on essential theoretical knowledge. Participants were tasked with completing the e-learning before any in-person training. Now, the training has shifted from pure instruction to hands-on application of knowledge: sales agents engaged in role plays, applying what they learned online to mimic real-world sales interactions.

As a result, training time was drastically reduced from three days to one, leading to substantial financial savings. What's more, trainees could navigate the learning content at their own pace. They could self-assess before the training, easily identifying gaps in knowledge. They could later refer to e-learning to refresh their memory as needed.

Blending synchronous training with trainer-made asynchronous courses is a cost-effective way to boost learning. This blended approach, powered by EGL, is evident in the flipped classroom method. Leadership development programmes, onboarding training and technical or software training are other examples where this approach yields many benefits.

Translation and localization needs

Building on the previous example, imagine the intricate task of translating learning materials into 30 languages. It's not merely about translating words, it's about ensuring comprehension, as people digest complex ideas better in their native tongue. And beyond translation, there's a need for localization to align with local customs, values and regulations.

Many companies, from corporations to start-ups, employ a diverse workforce spread across various linguistic and cultural backgrounds. Addressing this diversity is crucial.

Here is where EGL shines. Many of our customers use our built-in automated translation software. It can translate content into 75 languages and the result is very effective. *But* the finishing touch needs to come from human expertise. With local SMEs, organizations can fine-tune translations and make necessary cultural adjustments. This ensures content is both linguistically accurate and culturally relevant.

With this strategy, learners are better equipped to understand and apply knowledge in their roles. Leveraging the power of EGL and the insights of local SMEs, businesses can effectively bridge the language and cultural gaps, ensuring universally accessible and resonant training.

IT'S HARD TO MAKE IT EASY

The realizations around EGL not only had a significant impact on our customers, they also caused a transformative shift for our company and product. Before we embraced EGL, our primary offering was an authoring tool for instructional designers. To be distinctive in the instructional design tool market, you must have more features, arguably better ones, than your competitors. This means more interactions, diverse methods to present content and additional features – essentially a 'more is better' philosophy. Being in this competitive environment led to a race for features with our competitors. A significant downside was that these tools, ours included, became increasingly complex. Users needed extensive training to learn all the features. For instructional designers, whose main job is to develop learning content, mastering such an intricate tool might seem justifiable. *This is not the case with SMEs.* Their primary focus isn't on creating learning and support content, it's more of a side task derived from their responsibilities. They need a straightforward, intuitive and user-friendly tool, preferably with no learning curve – the opposite of the feature-rich tool we had at first.

The difference between an authoring tool for instructional designers and one for SMEs was so stark that we decided to build an entirely new tool. The goal was to have a tool with *no learning curve at all*, so merely simplifying our old one was not enough. We had to start from scratch, which was exciting. From a business perspective, it meant a 180-degree turn on everything: marketing, sales, partnerships, pricing, business model, customers and customer support. Every aspect required a fresh approach, distinct from our previous methods. And achieving simplicity in our product was much more complicated than I had expected.

The cornerstone of a tool without a steep learning curve lies in its top-notch, intuitive user interface (UI) and user experience (UX). I remember our discussions 10 years ago when we laid the foundations of our current solution. How could we design a UI so simple? We decided that a drag-and-drop interface would be best. Major decisions like this require thorough research for validation, so we scoured the market for learning authoring tools featuring a drag-and-drop mechanism. We couldn't find a single one. But we were so convinced of this choice that we went for it anyway. Today, our drag-and-drop feature is still one of our key selling points.

We created an interface segmented by tabs to divide the creation process and functionalities into smaller, more manageable portions. This added a clear process flow to the tool. Of course, that was just the beginning and there was much more to be done. It's been a highly exciting journey that taught us a lot. Now we're a platform where SMEs can create learning and performance content without any experience, prior knowledge or training.

We constantly review the UI and UX to ensure they stay simple and intuitive, making weekly improvements. The main lesson learned from all of this is that it is not only hard to make things easy, you must be truly committed to keeping it easy as well. That might be even harder.

The impact of EGL on L&D roles

EGL is a new way of creating learning and performance content. It enables tapping into your employees' expertise, fostering peer-to-peer learning and offering a fresh approach to L&D.

Among the largest customers of Easygenerator, only a small portion of their learning content is created or managed by L&D. In fact, a notable company in the food and beverage sector states that merely 5 per cent of their learning content is top-down – defined as mandatory materials crafted by the L&D department and instructional designers, then disseminated to learners via an LMS. This implies that a staggering 95 per cent of the content is authored by

SMEs and predominantly housed on an LXP, a platform where learners themselves determine their learning needs.

This departure from the traditional top-down method signifies a transformative shift for instructional designers and L&D departments. Moving away from a controlling role, L&D shifts towards co-creating, quality assurance, managing and coaching roles.

The co-creating role

EGL doesn't signify the end of content creation by instructional designers. Their specialized skills and knowledge in instructional design remain invaluable. But to get the benefits of EGL in terms of content production efficiency and cost-effectiveness, they must refrain from content creation and maintenance. In the EGL framework, instructional designers adopt a co-creation role, emphasizing the course's structural and didactic elements rather than raw content production. This collaboration can cover areas such as defining course objectives or laying out content structures. The *creation* role is always with the SMEs.

The quality assurance role

The second key role of the instructional designer is to ensure the quality of courses – not the content itself but rather from a didactical standpoint. The instructional designer's strength lies in understanding how to effectively transfer knowledge. Thus, their expertise is applied to refine and enhance content throughout its creation and post-creation processes.

In a 2022 study we did on SME content creation behaviours, we observed that SMEs often start the content creation process without defining a clear learning objective for their course. They share the knowledge they think would be useful to their peers, with little regard to direction or organization. And since they're not experts in didactics, this is completely normal. But it can result in lengthy and unengaging courses. This is where instructional designers play a crucial role. They direct SMEs in setting a clear objective from the start. Later, they make sure that each page covers a single concept. They break down lengthy modules into manageable segments, incorporate visuals where appropriate and even integrate quizzes to reinforce learning.

The management role

Another crucial responsibility of the instructional designer is content oversight. They ensure comprehensive coverage of essential topics, identifying and addressing any content gaps by collaborating with relevant SMEs. They also keep tabs on what's being created and whether it's published in the correct system. Beyond this, instructional designers streamline the entire content life cycle, from content creation to publication and maintenance. Their management ensures content is published accurately and remains current.

The coaching role

The impact on the work of instructional designers is, without a doubt, significant. Cumulatively, all these roles evolve the instructional designer from a content creator to an instructional coach for bottom-up learning initiatives – from content ownership to guidance. The focus becomes mentoring SMEs to help them produce didactically robust and effective learning materials.

The instructional designer, now acting as a coach, helps connect the dots by training SMEs on basic e-learning practices. This can be a virtual bootcamp or a resource that covers anything from understanding knowledge gaps to crafting content and making it visually interesting. They provide SMEs with tools, including content templates, style guides and media materials, along with easy-to-use creator tools. In addition, they provide regular feedback for ongoing improvement, sticking with SMEs throughout the process. This coaching role makes sure everything is up to par by checking regularly and thoroughly, making the whole content creation experience

FIGURE 3.4 Instructional designers and SMEs learning diagram

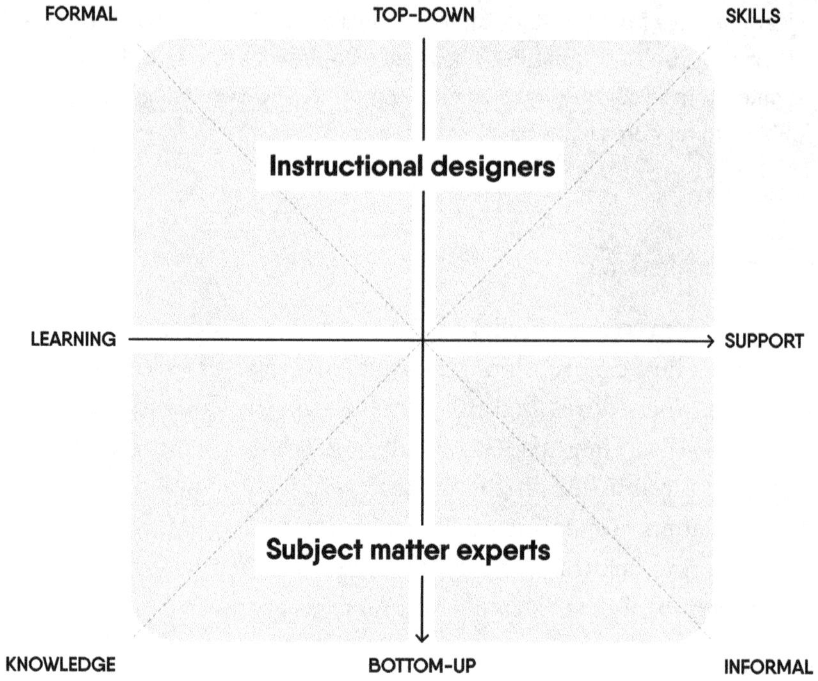

easy and seamless for the SMEs, so that they are inspired to continue sharing their knowledge as content.

When we visualize all these roles on the learning diagram, the distinctions become clear (see Figure 3.4). The upper half of the diagram, encompassing formal learning and competency development projects, often falls under the purview of the L&D department. Here, instructional designers frequently take the lead, designing and creating content with input from SMEs. This content, characterized by its top-down approach, is typically delivered to learners via LMSs.

Conversely, the lower half of the diagram, which represents knowledge sharing and workplace learning, primarily features content crafted by SMEs. This content is made accessible in an LXP, enabling learners to access it on demand, as per their needs. While it's feasible for content created by instructional designers to be published in an LXP and for SME-generated content to appear in an LMS, there's a natural alignment: top-half content gravitates towards LMSs while bottom-half content finds its place in LXPs.

Notes

1 Cujba, S (2023) How long does it take to create an online course?, Raccoon Gang. Available at: https://raccoongang.com/blog/how-long-does-it-take-create-online-course/ (archived at https://perma.cc/B3Q6-HZEW)

2 Movchan, S (2023) How much does it cost to develop an online course?, Raccoon Gang. Available at: https://raccoongang.com/blog/how-much-does-it-cost-create-online-course/ (archived at https://perma.cc/8J3P-VEA5)

3 Bersin, J (2022) The creator market for corporate learning: A massive, still untapped market, The Joshbersin Company, joshbersin.com/wp-content/uploads/2022/04/L_D-04_22-The-Creator-Market-for-Corporate-Learning-Report-v2.pdf (archived at https://perma.cc/JB53-H5KG)

4 Puddifoot, L (2021) Quote, Easygenerator's internal interview.

5 Shabatura, J (2022) Using Bloom's Taxonomy to write effective learning outcomes | Teaching innovation and pedagogical support. Available at: https://tips.uark.edu/using-blooms-taxonomy/#:~:text=Bloom 's%20Taxonomy%20is%20a%20classification%20of%20the%20different%20outcomes%20and,at%20the%20University%20of%20Chicago (archived at https://perma.cc/FA5H-ZYDZ)

6 Chui, M *et al.* (2012a) The Social Economy: Unlocking value and productivity through social technologies, McKinsey & Company. Available at: https://www.mckinsey.com/industries/technology-media-and-telecommunications/our-insights/the-social-economy (archived at https://perma.cc/4TSM-VQ4W) (Accessed: 21 August 2023).

7 Fellay, M (2021) Why your employees are leaving en masse and the surprising factor that will keep them, Forbes. Retrieved from https://www.forbes.com/sites/forbestechcouncil/2021/07/28/why-your-employees-are-leaving-en-masse-and-the-surprising-factor-that-will-keep-them/?sh=536885a40fbd (archived at https://perma.cc/8WQG-ZBAG)

8 World Economic Forum (2023) The Great Resignation continues. Why are US workers continuing to quit their jobs?, https://www.weforum.org/agenda/2023/01/us-workers-jobs-quit/ (archived at https://perma.cc/UF7A-WBTQ)

9 Adecco USA (2022) The Great Retirement: Are Baby Boomers causing today's hiring shortage?, blog.adeccousa.com/2022-hiring-trend-great-retirement/ (archived at https://perma.cc/B3V2-VSZM)

10 Bergmann, J and Sams, A (2012) *Flip Your Classroom: Reach every student in every class every day*, USA: International Society for Tech in Ed.

4

Theories (how we learn to work)

We started implementing Employee-generated Learning in 2013, so it's still a relatively new concept. But the theories that EGL is rooted in are well-established and time-tested learning models. By drawing from these, we not only solidified the foundation of EGL but found avenues to refine and expand its horizons. This chapter delves into the learning theories that underpin EGL, offering insights into its didactical origins, its evolutionary journey and its potential future.

The social dimension: social learning theories

The EGL model leverages the expertise and knowledge of employees, making them not just consumers but also producers of knowledge. Typically, these insights are shared with co-workers in similar roles, fostering an environment where knowledge transfer is organic and seamless. The magic of EGL is magnified when multiple SMEs collaborate, weaving their insights into a collective tapestry of knowledge.

When examining this model through the lens of socio-educational psychologists who believe that learning is deeply rooted in a social context, the parallels become apparent. Let's begin with John Dewey, an educational reformer. One of the key elements of his theories is that people develop and grow as they interact with the world. According to him, shared activities are a vital context for learning and development. People find new ideas and learn about new concepts and practices by interacting with their surroundings.[1] This perspective aligns perfectly with EGL's approach for learners. But as we delved deeper, we discovered that Dewey's philosophy is equally relevant to those authoring EGL content.

For the author, content creation is also a learning process. Creation is, after all, the highest level of learning of Bloom's Taxonomy (refer to Figure 3.3). And this is so true. When we set out to write this book, our initial thought was to document all we had learned about EGL over the past decade, but the process proved to be much more intricate. Sharing our knowledge and insights may have been the starting point of this book, but the moment we started writing it all down, many things began to happen. We noticed that some parts were incomplete. We reread sources and discovered that some notions could be interpreted differently. We suddenly noticed connections between certain elements we were unaware of before. We discovered gaps in the storyline, found inconsistencies and realized that some parts didn't even make much sense. We learned so much while writing this book, and these learning moments became our great motivators in completing it. It wasn't just writing down our experiences, it quickly became an exciting and insightful learning journey.

An essential aspect to consider when implementing EGL is the learning journey inherent in content creation. Often, this is overlooked. Navigating the learning process alone is almost impossible. In the best-case scenario, it will be only partially complete and impactful. Both learning and content creation are intrinsically social activities, amplifying the learning experience. We had the privilege of co-writing this book. Although we come from diverse backgrounds and experiences, our shared vision became a unifying force. Together, we brainstormed, challenged one another and introduced new perspectives. By blending our unique backgrounds, we enhanced the content. We used our different backgrounds to our advantage. When embracing EGL tools or processes, it's vital to foster a collaborative work and learning environment. Collaboration is the key element of learning and content creation.

For organizations, the key activity is bringing together experts on a particular domain, getting them to share knowledge and creating content together. When instructional designers create content, the major challenge is that they get their information from various sources, which can often be conflicting. This results in inconsistent and disparate e-learning courses. But when SMEs work together, they resolve any differences of opinion before putting pen to paper. They exchange ideas and produce unified, consistent content. Not only does this result in better e-learning, it also helps SMEs grow and learn.

The social learning aspect also applies to the content. Returning to this book as an example: together we wrote a book that neither of us could have done alone. The result is significantly better than if either of us had written it alone. And you, the reader of this book, will also have insights and experiences that will challenge, enhance and improve our ideas and content. That is why we organized a feedback loop for our readers. We want to learn from you. We invite you to become a part of improving this book. Reach out to us by visiting our website for this book at www.employeegeneratedlearning.com. Organizing a feedback loop with your readers or learners is crucial for creating high-value content, which also goes for EGL content. The moment of publication is only the beginning of the content's life cycle. It is by no means the end of the creation process.

This social and collaborative component is also in Vygotsky's concept of the zone of proximal development.[2] This theory describes how we learn from our social environment and use skilled peers to help us overcome learning challenges. Vygotsky states that you can only learn so much without the aid of a more experienced and accomplished person. In other words, the zone of proximal development refers to the additional learning that comes with guidance or support from a more experienced peer.

This is an interesting notion in the light of EGL. EGL content is a form of aided learning that expands learners' growth. But as with all content, that impact is less than being exposed to the source of that content, the people, the experts. Certainly, EGL content broadens the zone of proximal development. Yet imagine the deeper understanding one could attain if they were to directly interact with the expert. Such an exchange would involve learning by example and receiving hands-on coaching. This sparked a thought: if top SMEs took on coaching roles, their educational impact might surpass that of just sharing knowledge through content. Furthermore, having your experts devote some of their time to coaching, rather than solely focusing on frontline tasks, could elevate the overall performance of your company. Junior employees would gain invaluable experience by working alongside company SMEs, absorbing knowledge through hands-on experience.

Albert Bandura's social learning theory underscores the potential value of this master–apprentice dynamic. His work explores the impact of both contextual and cognitive elements on people's learning process. He states that we learn through observation, imitation and modelling, and that attention, motivation, attitudes and emotions influence learning.[3] These things are difficult to achieve if you have to learn from content alone; you need to learn from someone to make this happen. For maximum impact, learning needs to occur in the context of work – not in the context of learning.

Because of this, we now have the notion that the next level of learning from experts, the next level of EGL, could be in coaching. This extended idea of EGL is connected closely to the master–apprentices theories and practices. It is a potential way of returning that form of learning to corporate learning. Presumably, you'll not only enhance your learning and coaching programmes but also boost your organization's performance. We work out this idea in greater detail in the book's final chapter, where we investigate the future of EGL.

> Creating EGL is a collaborative learning process between co-authors, as well as between authors and learners. By introducing a coaching system or a master–apprentice structure, we can elevate this learning within the workplace. EGL enables apprentices to become new masters, disseminating knowledge, insights and experiences. In doing so, they pave the way for the next generation of experts to both create content and mentor subsequent generations. We see this as the future of scalable and applicable corporate learning. EGL plays a vital role in establishing this infrastructure.

Situated workplace learning theories: context

Context is vital in any social learning theory or initiative. In the corporate world, this primarily means the workplace. It's essential that learning initiatives are deeply connected to the workplace setting for meaningful corporate learning. The environment in which we learn greatly affects the success of our learning efforts. Context is everything.

For social learning interactions to be effective, learners and their knowledgeable peers should engage in real-world situations. Without the right context, learning experiences might not be as powerful. Many learning theories support this. Prominent learning theories, such as the theory of situated cognition, highlight the importance of context in learning.[4] It suggests that people learn best by participating in activities alongside experts in their field and engaging in social interactions. It advocates that real learning occurs in the same authentic context in which it will be applied and that knowledge is only truly acquired when it is applied. It can't be retained if learned independently. This points to the need for integrating learning and content creation directly into the workplace environment, a fundamental aspect of EGL. This is also why SMEs, *not* instructional designers, should be at the forefront of creating learning content.

The inception of EGL was driven by the instructional designers' evident disconnect from business context. This lack of context is exactly why the formal learning process has limitations. It's also one of the critical issues with our educational system, though that's a topic for another book.

Another socio-educational theory from Malcolm Knowles' Six Principles of Andragogy emphasizes that adults are self-directed. They're interested in learning subjects that are immediately relevant to their work or personal lives.[5] This means that adult learning should be problem-centred rather than content-oriented. It should focus on practical application. This is quite similar to situated learning, which emphasizes the need to learn in the context of authentic work-related tasks rather than remote training sessions.

These theories all steer us towards problem-centred, social learning within the workplace context, which is precisely what microlearning can bring. Before moving on, we need to clarify what we mean by microlearning. While there are many definitions, we define it as workplace learning that can be consumed while working. It helps solve a problem or issue encountered while working. Examples include best practices, how-to guides and FAQs. Microlearning promotes problem-solving or solution-focused education, and is vital for introducing learning in the workplace and fostering a rich, context-based learning experience. This isn't an EGL-specific conclusion; it goes for all learning. To be effective, L&D programmes should focus on solving real-world problems and allow learners to apply their knowledge in practical (preferably workplace) settings. When you implement corporate learning this way, learning becomes embedded in everyday work. We should stop talking about increasing learner engagement and motivation or improving learning outcomes. These are remedies for a bad learning approach and bad learner motivation. They're not fundamental improvements of corporate learning; they are patchwork at best.

EGL offers a practical approach to applying these theories. It helps establish a learning environment that aligns with these ideas and is key to effective job performance. EGL allows experienced professionals to pass on their practical knowledge and skills to those less experienced. The main goal is sharing job-specific knowledge that has been tested and proven through personal experience.

When the sharing of knowledge and experience is expanded and maintained consistently, it nurtures an environment where individuals can learn from one another. Such an environment can lead to the formation of a community of practice. A community of practice, as defined by Lave and Wenger in 1991, is a group of people with a shared interest who come together to learn and share their experiences.[6] This is beneficial for businesses, as it promotes the sharing of best practices, encourages problem solving and supports the development of new skills. Beyond that, it helps in coming up with new solutions. In this collaborative setting, new ideas are generated and challenges are addressed. However, when the shared objectives are achieved, communities of practices typically dissolved as the unifying interest fades away. The knowledge gained during this time typically remains with the participants. Therefore, connecting a community of practice to an EGL content creation effort can ensure that the insights and knowledge are documented and made available to a wider audience. This idea will be explored further in the final chapter of this book.

When considering the content needed for the learning initiatives we've touched on, there's a need for both structured courses and microlearning. This leads us to one of the contemporary theories we find influential: the '5 moments of learning need' by Conrad Gottfredson and Bob Mosher, creators of the 5 Moments of Needs framework.[7] As the name suggests, these moments highlight when an individual feels the need to learn. Gottfredson and Mosher identified five specific times when this need arises:

1 When you learn something for the first time (**new**).
2 When you want to learn more about something (**more**).
3 When you try to apply and/or remember the thing you learned (**apply**).
4 When something goes wrong (**solve**).
5 When you have to deal with change (**change**).

Making a distinction between these moments and their connected learning needs will help you solve these needs more efficiently. This theory also helps determine when to use a formal learning approach, such as a course or classroom, or if a more informal option, like microlearning or coaching, is more effective.

In Figure 4.1, the five moments of learning needs are plotted onto the three phases you must go through to become a competent worker: *train*, *transfer* and *sustain*.

The first learning moment, *new*, occurs when you encounter a concept or task for the first time. *More* is when you have a basic understanding of the topic but need to deepen your knowledge or skills substantially. *New* and *more* are part of the *train* phase. You need to acquire a lot of information in a relatively short time span. These needs

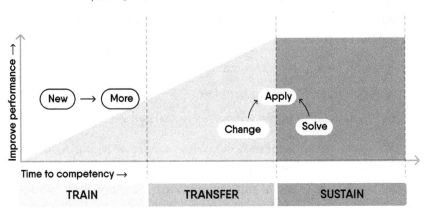

can be addressed with a formal learning approach: face-to-face training, e-learning modules or a blended approach. In the figure, knowledge gain is represented as the shaded regions that get wider as you go from left to right. By using the knowledge and developing skills during the *training and transfer* phases, we become better at our jobs. We slowly grow into a fully competent worker. Once we achieve that, we move to the *sustain* phase, where we aim to keep that level of skill.

The five stages of learning present an interesting parallel with Maslow's theory, which outlines the four stages of competency:[8]

First stage: First, you need to know what you must learn. Maslow calls this 'unconsciously incompetent'. At this stage, in his words, you are 'ignorant'.

Second stage: After the initial training, you know what you must do but can't execute yet. You are 'consciously incompetent'. You are aware of your incompetence; this coincides with the beginning of the *transfer* phase.

Third stage: Over time, you become 'consciously competent', which means you can perform the task but are still learning.

Fourth stage: Finally, when you are so competent that you can perform the task without giving it a thought, you are 'unconsciously competent' – you've mastered the skill. Getting from 'unconsciously incompetent' to 'unconsciously competent' requires a lot of training and experiences.

During the *transfer and sustain* phases, you progress through four stages: from being unconsciously unskilled to unconsciously skilled. As you navigate these stages, different learning needs arise, all while you are on the job:

- When you encounter a **change**.
- When you need to **solve** a problem.
- When you need to **apply** what you've learned before.

But you want to fulfil these needs while you're working; you don't want to stop working to attend training or watch an e-learning course. You want to find a solution and swiftly resume your work. In these cases, moments of learning needs aren't addressed with formal learning but by digestible performance support.

While *new* and *more* learning moments require formal learning, the rest require workplace learning, which is support. This division in learning needs helps us to decide what learning or support content we should offer a course or a performance support resource. It's another driver for adding performance support content to EGL.

All of this reflection helps determine what type of content you need to support the people in your company. Cathy Moore takes it one step further with her action mapping theory.[9] She believes that learning objectives should not only align with business goals but also prompt a change in behaviour. It's not enough just to acquire knowledge in a business setting. Moore emphasizes that knowledge must be put into action. You should be able to do something new or differently. While there's a lot more to her action mapping theory, what stood out to us was her emphasis on 'action'. Moore suggests a modification in the conventional five moments of learning needs. Instead of seeing 'apply' as merely a learning need, she sees it as a fundamental component of all learning. Thus, she advocates for the *four* moments of learning needs:

- New and apply.
- More and apply.
- Change and apply.
- Solve and apply.

Moore's approach connects learning to business goals, emphasizing real-world actions over just gaining knowledge. For us, this was another push in the direction of action-oriented microlearning. But it also inspired us further. When we looked at courses made by SMEs, they often had too much information and not enough practical application. Too content-heavy, too wordy. Most SMEs created such content because that was the kind of learning material they were used to seeing.

We needed to make them aware that they should look at content creation in a different way. We encourage SMEs to make shorter, focused microlearning content. To help with this, we introduced a tool in Easygenerator: Outline Builder, which is a course outline generator. The idea was simple; courses should be about doing things, not just knowing things. With the Outline Builder, authors could plan content that met their colleagues' real-world needs. They were prompted to think about the real challenges their content would solve and to give clear examples. The tool then generated a course plan full of actionable steps.

We've built our approach and tools around Moore's ideas, pushing for learning that's both practical and direct. We also wanted to help SMEs pick the right content, steering them towards what's essential for the task at hand. This usually meant shorter, more focused courses without any unnecessary information. The outline tool helped create a course plan that matched this goal. Our aim was to move SMEs towards making content that leads to action. By doing this, we've incorporated Cathy Moore's ideas into both our strategy and our software.

Notes

1 Dewey, J (1938) *Experience and Education*, New York: Collier Books.
2 Vygotsky, L S (1978) *Mind in Society: The development of higher psychological processes*, Cambridge, MA: Harvard University Press.
3 Bandura, A (1977) *Social Learning Theory*, Englewood Cliffs, NJ: Prentice Hall.
4 Lave, J and Wenger, E (1991) *Situated Learning: Legitimate peripheral participation*, Cambridge, UK: Cambridge University Press.

5 Knowles, M S (1980) *The Modern Practice of Adult Education: From pedagogy to andragogy*, New York: Cambridge Adult Education.

6 Lave, J and Wenger, E (1991) *Situated Learning: Legitimate peripheral participation*, Cambridge, UK: Cambridge University Press.

7 Mosher, B and Gottfredson, C (2011) *Innovative Performance Support: Strategies and practices for learning in the workflow*, San Francisco, CA: Wiley.

8 Broadwell, M M (1969) Teaching for learning, https://rider-ed.com/wp-content/uploads/2019/03/Four-Stages-of-Competence.pdf (archived at https://perma.cc/H6NF-M6PG)

9 Moore, C (2017) *Map It: The hands-on guide to strategic training design*, Romania: Montesa Press.

5

Employee-generated Learning and different content types

We delved into learning theories to understand the underpinnings of Employee-generated Learning, its driving factors and potential directions. Central to EGL is content creation and maintenance. The big question is: which content is ideal for EGL and which should be created by L&D teams? We began addressing this in Chapter 3, where we outlined the six criteria to identify the best content type for various scenarios.

This provides some insight into distinguishing between topics suited for an EGL approach and those less appropriate for it. Notably, the research conducted by RedThread on corporate learning content is highly useful.[1] They formulated the Learning Content Model based on their findings, illustrated in Figure 5.1.

The Learning Content Model consists of a four-quadrant diagram. The first axis ranges from *specific to generic*, representing the uniqueness of content to an organization. The second axis spans from *durable to perishable*, indicating the content's shelf life. These two criteria from RedThread, durability and specificity, are quite similar to the 'subject and speed of change' criteria mentioned in Table 5.1. We agree that of the six criteria we've mentioned, these two are the most influential. RedThread employs this model to decide, in their terms, 'what content should be overseen by the L&D function and what can be delegated or entrusted to other members of the organization'. This mirrors one of the key questions when assessing EGL's

TABLE 5.1 EGL vs L&D-generated content

	L&D-generated	Employee-generated
Target audience size	Impacts more than 12.5% of your workforce	Impacts less than 12.5% of your workforce
Target audience geography	Global	Regional or local or specific projects
Priority for L&D	Top 10	Not top 10
Stakeholder level	Senior leadership	Directors and below
Subject	Generic content like security and compliance	Business-specific topics
Speed of change	Low	High

suitability. The secondary question is: who takes charge of content creation and upkeep? We'll use the RedThread model to address both these inquiries within the context of the four quadrants. RedThread characterizes the quadrants as:

1 **Specific & durable**: Learning content that's unique to one organization. This type of content has a long shelf life. L&D teams should control the planning and creation of this type of content.

2 **Specific & perishable**: Learning content unique to one organization but changes often. L&D teams should *enable* creating this content but not create or control it.

3 **Generic & perishable**: Learning content that applies to many organizations and often changes. L&D teams should help employees filter out the right content from existing sources.

4 **Generic & durable**: Learning content that applies to many organizations. This content type also has a long shelf life. L&D teams should make this content available by purchasing libraries of this kind of content and publishing it on their learning platforms.

The model clarifies the roles of L&D teams and SMEs in managing and producing these four kinds of content. However, in the context of EGL, we believe there's room to delve deeper. We'll start by

FIGURE 5.1 The Learning Content Model (adapted from RedThread)

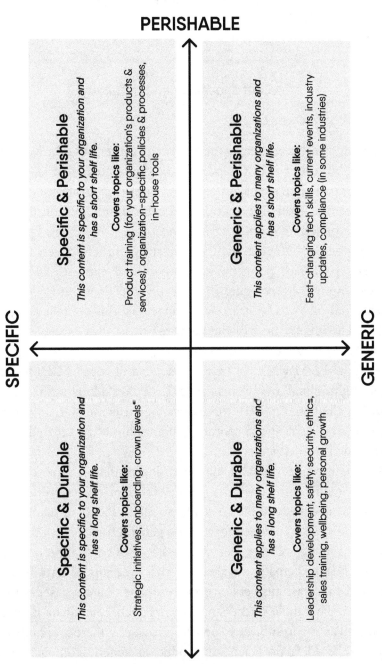

PERISHABLE

SPECIFIC

GENERIC

DURABLE

Specific & Perishable

This content is specific to your organization and has a short shelf life.

Covers topics like:
Product training (for your organization's products & services), organization-specific policies & processes, in-house tools

Generic & Perishable

This content applies to many organizations and has a short shelf life.

Covers topics like:
Fast-changing tech skills, current events, industry updates, compliance (in some industries)

Specific & Durable

This content is specific to your organization and has a long shelf life.

Covers topics like:
Strategic initiatives, onboarding, crown jewels*

Generic & Durable

This content applies to many organizations and has a long shelf life.

Covers topics like:
Leadership development, safety, security, ethics, sales training, wellbeing, personal growth

*Crown jewels refer to intellectual property that is critical to success or provides a competitive advantage to the company.

discussing these axes and then explore the four content categories through an EGL lens.

Content specificity and durability

Specific versus generic content

Company-specific content is the bread and butter of EGL. We already spoke a bit about it in Chapter 3. It's the content that's unique to your company and stems directly from your organization's expertise. Typically, this is the information you can't simply pull off a shelf or find in a generic course. It's vital and often proprietary. Under the EGL model, it's created swiftly, efficiently and effectively. It is the ultimate source of performance support and captures and retains critical, unique knowledge. It preserves the organization's unique intellectual assets. The primary architects of this content should be SMEs. The involvement of the L&D team can vary across organizations. Some may have a more structured EGL process, needing more input from L&D, while others may have a more open EGL approach, requiring minimal involvement from L&D. We'll look at this in more detail in Chapter 7, where we discuss the different EGL approaches. In both cases, specific corporate content should be created by and maintained by SMEs.

On the flip side, much of the e-learning content is generic – applicable to many companies. It's neither efficient nor cost-effective to create this in-house, so there's really no point. Plenty of readily available resources and courses cover these general topics. With the rise of AI, including ChatGPT, generating this type of content becomes even easier. These systems comb through vast amounts of data from the web and can craft answers or even complete courses based on what they find. This makes accessing average web content or prevailing perspectives on a subject a breeze. However, there's a cautionary note: while AI is proficient at producing generic content, it's still crucial to verify the accuracy. Just because something is online doesn't mean it's correct.

While L&D teams create a lot of generic learning material, companies tend not to follow generic theories or approaches for all their training needs. In our experience, it's best to complement generically produced content with small additions specific to the company. You can also create a small addendum course focusing only on your company specifics and deviations. Adding this EGL layer makes the content relevant to your organization.

> At Easygenerator we have a methodology called *scaling up*.[2] It's a method that helps companies to grow fast but in a healthy and balanced way. Our employees can either read the book or take one of the generic courses on scaling up. We have also made an Easygenerator course that outlines how we do it at our company. The combination of generic learning material and the specific learning content is an effective approach for any type of team training.

Durable versus perishable content

The speed of business is increasing, meaning learning content must be updated more often. This means the shelf life of content is diminishing. But this isn't true for all content – only perishable content is affected, while durable content stands the test of time.

When it comes to perishable content, it's best for SMEs to handle its creation and maintenance. Given their close ties to the business, they are more attuned to real-time changes and can adapt content accordingly. However, this doesn't mean that L&D teams and instructional designers should be the sole creators of durable content. Quite the contrary, in fact. Even for long-standing content, the SME is often the individual best equipped to evaluate its continued relevance. They have a deep understanding of the subject and can assess and integrate changes into training materials, ensuring that even the most durable content remains current and beneficial.

Classification of content

The two axes that we discussed define the four quadrants. Now, let's take a look at each of these quadrants.

Specific and durable

Organization-specific learning and support content tends to have a long shelf life. For example, subjects like company values or DEIB (diversity, equity, inclusion and belonging) belong to this category. RedThread has recommended that L&D should align this type of content with organizational initiatives or create sticky content to steer the related initiatives.[3] But when viewed through the lens of EGL, there are some nuances to consider. While it's appropriate for L&D teams to coordinate and ensure this content is available, they shouldn't necessarily be the ones crafting and updating it. That responsibility better lies with the SMEs. The role of L&D, then, is more about pinpointing the right SMEs, allocating tasks, offering guidance and supporting them throughout the process, rather than generating the content directly.

For example, take a formal e-learning course, *Company History and Milestones*. This type of specific, enduring content is typically crafted by the L&D department. Now, picture whether such a resource, be it a course, whitepaper, video or book, was penned by the company's founder (just as this book was). While it remains a valuable educational asset, it wouldn't be under the purview of the L&D department. This is more about sharing knowledge, and the founder, who knows the most about the subject, should lead it. (In this case, the founder is the SME.) At the same time, we should remember that employees can share their own unique experiences too. Observing it in this light, the content envelops several segments of our learning diagram: formal learning, competency development, knowledge sharing and experience sharing. While the knowledge all relates to the same specific and enduring topic, the content can take many forms, each with a different owner and creation process.

This also applies to learning content on organizational values and culture. Most companies likely have formal courses on their values and company culture. This information is specific, durable and, at first glance, suited to be an L&D-owned topic. But knowledge sharing is important here as well. Employees who embody these values can be living examples of this content's essence.

Usually, most organizations' onboarding programmes include some sort of training on organizational values and company values. A helpful strategy to reinforce this is assigning a coworker or 'buddy' to newcomers during their initial days. If this buddy exemplifies the company's values, they can effectively demonstrate their significance to the new hire. Such a buddy could be a seasoned employee, possibly an SME. At first, this initiative would be SME-led given the *specific* nature of the content. But over time, as the content becomes more generic and applicable to a broader audience, the topic can get integrated into L&D's broader effort to familiarize everyone with the company values.

Alternatively, let's examine a course on strategy or product vision. This type of content falls into the specific and durable category because the strategic direction or product vision doesn't frequently change. It has a long shelf life. In this scenario, it is unlikely that the L&D team would have the expertise or authority to manage or update the course content fully. The subject remains under the purview of the SMEs with the specialized knowledge and insights required to keep it relevant and up to date.

Learning content comes in many shapes. It doesn't necessarily have to be a course, microlearning or performance support. At Easygenerator, we have a value recognition channel on Slack. We hold four core corporate values and to highlight these we've developed digital postcards. These postcards feature notable quotes from renowned individuals that align with and emphasize these values.

Whenever a team member exemplifies a company value through a notable action or accomplishment, we celebrate them on the channel. We include a postcard, tag them and describe what they did and why it was so great.

> This not only publicly acknowledges the team member, it also provides real-time, practical examples of how these values can be embodied in our daily work. It's powerful learning material. Such real-world stories, shared directly by colleagues, can arguably be more impactful in teaching our values than e-learning or training. The added benefit is the constant stream of new stories that people share. This creates a lively and updated source of content that everyone sees and engages with.
>
> Based on the learning content diagram, values typically fall into the *specific and durable* category. But this example shows that *specific and perishable* information can also be very valuable. While the primary learning content aligns perfectly with a specific quadrant, it's also important to incorporate relevant materials from other quadrants. In other words, to achieve a larger goal, it can be vital to bring together learning materials from different quadrants.

Specific and perishable

Unique content that is specific to an organization and frequently changes, such as product information, falls under the category of specific and perishable. RedThread argues that L&D teams shouldn't create or control this content and we agree.[4] Indeed, it's not suitable for the L&D team to own and produce content of this nature.

> When a company rolls out a new product or service, there's an immediate need for training materials that detail its features, advantages and usage protocols. Yet the shelf life of this content is short-lived. Whereas in the past updates might have been annual or biannual occurrences, the modern tempo, particularly in SaaS firms, often sees products being refreshed on a weekly basis, if not more frequently. This directly influences the relevancy and accuracy of such training materials.

The trend of 'continuous deployment', where features, updates, improvements or bug fixes are released as soon as they're completed, makes it unfeasible for the L&D team to manage this type of content. Only those closely involved in product updates can keep the training materials for product information updated. Adding to this challenge, L&D departments are struggling with growing backlogs. Many learning requests are about very specific topics for highly specialized, small audiences. This is due to the increased specialization and internationalization of organizations. We argue that such specific content shouldn't even make its way to L&D's backlog. The L&D team will likely lack the necessary expertise and, crucially, the limited audience for these specialized courses won't warrant the intensive time and effort commitment. The investment simply outweighs the returns. Specific and perishable content should be created and maintained by SMEs.

Generic and perishable

This type of content is broadly applicable yet frequently changing. Examples include market data or various economic reports. RedThread suggests that L&D's role should be to steer employees towards already available, credible sources of this information.[5] While it's clear that companies shouldn't be recreating this kind of content, it's debatable whether L&D is best suited to curate or aid in curating this content.

The nuanced complexities of topics such as ever-evolving market trends – whether they pertain to competitor products, marketing tactics, sales strategies or the intricacies of market dynamics – demand SME insights. These trends constantly evolve, requiring close monitoring. In our view, L&D is not suited for this task – only experienced specialists can effectively sift through this information and identify trends. Therefore, L&D's role becomes even more indirect. Their duty is to ensure that the relevant SMEs are actively tracking this information and updating related content. And, to create environments where the content is created, maintained and made accessible to learners.

Generic and durable

In this quadrant, we discuss learning content that's widely applicable to many organizations *and* has a long shelf life. The first step is selecting third-party content on these topics. SMEs play a critical role here: they identify which content is most relevant for the company. L&D's role is to acquire this content, whether that means buying libraries or individual courses and then publishing them on the learning platforms. Note that while this content is durable, it can still be updated.

Examples of such content include topics like communication skills, problem-solving techniques and time management. These are all generic and long-lasting subjects. As mentioned before, this is the kind of content that generative AI can impact significantly. The use of AI to create these courses is now becoming an option. AI developments are happening rapidly. If you use an AI service to generate a course on a particular topic today, you'll get a well-organized outline. However, like all AI-generated content, it's essential to review and ensure its accuracy. The content might be dense and it might not follow all instructional design principles. This means AI-generated courses are a good starting point if you want to develop learning content, but they aren't ready to be published as they are.

Generic content and curation

There are different reasons for acquiring generic content. Sometimes, the desired content isn't available for free, or there's a need to ensure the right material is chosen. This naturally pivots such content towards the concept of curation.

Curation comes from the art world: a curator's role is to select and arrange art for exhibitions. Similarly, in the learning landscape, curation involves an SME choosing and organizing content or knowledge, ensuring its relevance and accuracy.

Opting for curation can be more effective than solely depending on search engines. Using general search tools might lead SMEs to inaccurate, outdated or even irrelevant content. Or, in some instances, the needed information might not be found at all. A potential remedy is purchasing the content, allowing its integration into an LMS for tracking purposes. The question is: do you need to track and trace these results? If the answer is no, curation is a solid alternative.

Curation is more nuanced than collecting information on a certain topic. It's much more than what a Google query can do. Curation is about intentional searching, rigorous selection and thoughtful presentation of content. While search tools can provide raw data, the SME refines – selecting and curating the most valuable pieces. Most importantly, effective curation is rooted in context. What is the purpose of curating this content, what is the goal and who is the audience? If you asked us for a list of e-learning resources, we could easily provide it. But without specifics, the list would be too broad. So instead of asking for 'a list of e-learning resources', you now ask for 'a list of e-learning resources for new hires who need to sell our authoring tool'. With clear boundaries, the list becomes purposeful and valuable.

This task of setting boundaries and ensuring purposeful curation falls on the shoulders of L&D. While SMEs choose or curate content based on their expertise, the L&D department offers direction, ensuring the process remains aligned with overarching goals.

Generic information should be curated or purchased – not created. If the purchased content doesn't fully cover your company- or team-specific insights, consider adding an addendum at the end.

Specific information should be created and maintained by SMEs.

Specific and durable content can be owned by L&D but should be created by or with SMEs. Examples include content on company history and milestones, organizational values and culture.

Specific and perishable content should be owned and created by SMEs. L&D should facilitate this process and ensure the content is available to everyone. Examples include product training and competitor insights.

Generic and perishable content should not be created, it should be acquired. SMEs should curate while L&D manages its boundaries and distribution.

Generic and durable content should be acquired by L&D and made available to the employees. SMEs will play a role in selecting the correct content. Examples are content on communication skills, problem-solving techniques, economic reports and time management.

Content types

The RedThread content framework, enriched with our unique EGL perspective, provides a robust foundation for structuring and categorizing diverse learning resources. This framework equips L&D professionals, trainers, SMEs and instructional designers with the insights needed to craft informed decisions during the learning content creation process.

To further enhance this understanding, we compiled a list of learning content types that organizations create. This list combines our insights[6] with those of other experts in the field, including Donald Taylor,[7] Clive Shepherd,[8] Nick Shackleton-Jones, Bob Mosher[9] and Conrad Gottfredson, and Marc Zao-Sanders.[10]

Supportive content

- **Reference content:** Manuals, job aids and documentation that provide step-by-step instructions or guidance.
- **Performance support content:** Resources designed to assist learners in real time while performing tasks; offers quick access to information, tools and resources.

Formal learning content

- **Learning resources:** Interactive e-learning modules, workshops and classroom training.
- **High-end content:** Unique and specialized e-learning content with complex objectives, incorporating elements such as intelligence, personalization, simulations, game play and rich media.

Social learning content

- **Social learning content:** Platforms and resources facilitating collaboration, knowledge sharing and engagement among learners, including discussion forums, online communities and social media platforms.

- **User-generated content/Employee-generated Learning:** Resources created and shared by learners or employees, encouraging active participation and knowledge exchange.

Informal learning content

- **Informal learning content:** Self-directed learning materials that can be accessed at learners' convenience, including blogs, articles, podcasts and videos.
- **Curated content/web content:** A selection of internal and external existing content organized so that others can access it. This includes curating web resources like articles, videos, images, documents, massive open online courses (MOOCs), blogs and podcasts.
- **Rapid development content:** Digital content created to quickly communicate simple information or provide basic knowledge through interactive tutorials, short videos, podcasts, screen captures, PowerPoint presentations or PDF files.

Additional content types

- **Bespoke e-learning creation:** Content created by instructional designers through employee interviews, tailoring the learning materials to specific organizational needs.
- **Off-the-shelf content:** Ready-made learning materials purchased from content marketplaces or suppliers.
- **Proprietary content:** Organization-specific content created internally, tailored to the workforce's needs – may have limited metadata quality.
- **Generic library content:** Paid content licensed by multiple organizations, including general-purpose, format-focused marketplaces, aggregators, MOOCs, specialists and web crawlers.

Now, let's map these different content types on the content quadrant. This sample mapping will help you distinguish the content types available at your organization and plan the learning interventions accordingly. Figure 5.2 is a sample visualization.

FIGURE 5.2 The Learning Content Diagram (adapted by RedThread) with examples

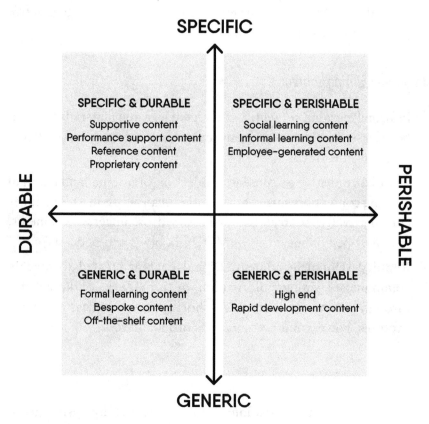

When you look at a particular topic, it's never covered by only one type of content. Even if a topic is primarily associated with one quadrant, it isn't restricted to that specific quadrant. For a single topic, there might be multiple documents, each of a different nature, possibly crafted by various owners. This means that it's the *character* of the content, rather than merely the topic, that dictates its placement within a quadrant.

New tools

In the early stages of e-learning, organizations used a one-size-fits-all LMS. The L&D department created and disseminated all official learning content to learners through the LMS. However, this chapter highlights the vast diversity in content, content creators and content owners. We need different tools to create this content and a solution more flexible than the traditional top-down LMS to deliver it effectively to learners and workers. You need a simple and intuitive authoring tool with no learning curve for content creation. Instead of the top-down LMS, you need more advanced systems to assist the worker in finding all this information in their moment of learning. Traditional LMSs cannot fulfil this need. While current LXPs and performance support tools do a better job than the old LMS, they still fall short. We see a significant role for AI here, not necessarily in content creation (a focus of generative AI) but more in organizing, contextualizing content and delivering it to the worker at the right time. We'll delve deeper into tools and their ongoing development in Chapter 8.

LEARNING BY DOING

Writing down these foundations of EGL was an exciting experience that helped us recognize our progress on our journey so far. In 2013, we set out to solve the typically slow and expensive content development process that plagued L&D departments. But it evolved into something so much bigger. We addressed issues like knowledge loss, translation and localization issues. We played a significant role in creating a whole new category of learning content with many of our clients. This journey has been a great example of *learning by doing*. All these applications and implications of EGL came up in conversations with our customers, which have greatly influenced our thinking, product and company.

The most impactful change over the past decade has been the introduction of microlearning. Realizing that SMEs can share knowledge in many ways other than e-learning courses, we added microlearning to our product: checklists, how-tos, best practices, frequently asked questions and even audio and video recordings. These make EGL a lot more accessible for SMEs. Creating a checklist is easier and faster than creating a complete e-learning course. So microlearning draws a whole new group of authors towards EGL – people who might otherwise be discouraged by the didactic challenge of creating e-learning. In hindsight, microlearning even could have been our starting point, but we were focused on improving the process of learning content creation.

Microlearning makes a new content category. It adds to the corporate brain and provides on-the-job performance support that helps people do their job better and faster. And although we are relatively at the beginning of this development as of 2023, its vast impact on corporate learning and EGL is already apparent. Microlearning is a real game-changer.

Notes

1 Adams, H G (2021) Learning Content. RedThread Research. Retrieved from https://redthreadresearch.com/learning-content/ (archived at https://perma.cc/6XBT-KGPP)

2 Harnish, V (2014) *Scaling Up: How a few companies make it... and why the rest don't* (Rockefeller Habits 2. 0), United States: Gazelles Incorporated.

3 Adams, H G (2022) Learning Content: Embracing the chaos, RedThread Research. Available at: https://redthreadresearch.com/learning-content/ (archived at https://perma.cc/8ZTM-N2F3) (Accessed: 23 August 2023).

4 Adams, H G (2022) Learning Content: Embracing the chaos, RedThread Research. Available at: https://redthreadresearch.com/learning-content/ (archived at https://perma.cc/Q3L3-TY9V) (Accessed: 23 August 2023).

5 Adams, H G (2022) Learning Content: Embracing the chaos, RedThread Research. Available at: https://redthreadresearch.com/learning-content/ (archived at https://perma.cc/7FQD-Z3RB) (Accessed: 23 August 2023).

6 Spiro, K (nd) The 4 tectonic shifts in L&D: Content creation, Easygenerator Blog. Retrieved from https://www.easygenerator.com/en/blog/authoring/4-tectonic-shifts-training-development-content-creation/ (archived at https://perma.cc/Y725-5A4G)

7 Taylor, D H (2017) 6 types of learning content, LinkedIn. Retrieved from https://www.linkedin.com/pulse/6-types-learning-content-donald-h-taylor/ (archived at https://perma.cc/K6GS-U42K)

8 Shepherd, C (2008) Three tiers in the content pyramid. Clive on learning. Retrieved from http://www.cliveonlearning.com/2008/06/three-tiers-in-content-pyramid.html (archived at https://perma.cc/VU7Q-U8M3)

9 Mosher, B (2017) Learning leaders: Bob Mosher advocates 'workflow learn-ing', *Learning Solutions Magazine*. Retrieved from https://www.learningguild.com/articles/2352/learning-leaders-bob-mosher-advocates-workflow-learning/ (archived at https://perma.cc/LZ79-NBLC)

10 Zao-Sanders, M (nd) The buyer's guide to learning content. Retrieved from https://learn.filtered.com/buyers-guide-learning-content#content-types (archived at https://perma.cc/YBX9-EJAS)

6

Regulated and democratized Employee-generated Learning

Over the last decade, we've worked with many customers, assisting them in the roll-out of Employee-generated Learning. Initially, our support was largely about helping them adopt the software. But along the way **we learned that implementing EGL in an organization is about more than just using an e-learning software.** It's an idea with the potential to reshape how people learn and work; it can influence and even change learning culture and, potentially, corporate culture. In this chapter, we'll share the lessons we have learned to help you benefit from our experience, ensuring a successful EGL roll-out in your organization and maximizing its impact.

The implementation of EGL varies for each organization, but we've identified two primary methods: the regulated approach and the democratized approach.

In *regulated* EGL, control over the content creation process stays with the L&D department. Their goal is to harness the advantages of EGL while maintaining oversight. They refine the existing content creation process. Here, instructional designers craft courses rooted in the central EGL concept: SMEs and those outside the traditional learning realm are responsible for both creating and updating content. As a result, the content creation process is enhanced and its reach is broadened. These SMEs now produce learning materials that the L&D department couldn't previously develop due to various reasons, like a lack of subject expertise.

Conversely, the *democratized* approach puts the SME in control. The primary aim here is to enable SMEs to share their knowledge widely, capturing their expertise and experiences for the benefit of their colleagues. Putting the SME in control isn't just a process improvement – it's an initiative to elevate productivity and work quality through shared knowledge.

We also learned that most organizations start with one of these approaches but that changes over time. An organization that starts out with a regulated approach to address content creation challenges might, over time, also adopt an EGL approach centred on knowledge sharing. Likewise, those beginning with EGL primarily for knowledge sharing might eventually leverage its advantages for content production. This suggests that in the long run, a blended model and a mixed implementation will often arise. We call this blended model the *managed democratized approach*.

Regulated EGL

In the regulated approach, the L&D department retains control over learning content creation. In practice, this means that the L&D department adheres as closely as possible to the traditional process of learning content creation. It starts with the L&D department identifying a learning need and deciding to create a course to solve that learning need. The conventional process can be outlined as follows:

1 Instructional designers conduct research. They define the audience, learning outcomes and objectives to start designing the course.

2 Since they lack the business knowledge to create content, the instructional designers interview SMEs to gather information. They often get conflicting information from different SMEs and need further research to determine the correct information.

3 Based on the interview research, the instructional designers design the course, create the content and have it reviewed by the SMEs.

4 The course undergoes a governance process and is published in the LMS or LXP.

5 The instructional designer is responsible for the course's maintenance after publication.

The method wherein the instructional designer is responsible for gathering content is time-consuming and incurs significant costs. Moreover, maintaining the accuracy and relevance of such content presents a big challenge. Since instructional designers aren't directly in tune with the dynamic business environment, they often lack real-time insights into changes in processes, best practices or evolving knowledge domains within the company. As a result, they may not be promptly aware of crucial updates that should be reflected in the learning content. The most practical solution they can often resort to is setting an expiration date for the course.

Using SMEs differently in combination with a regulated EGL approach can help solve these issues.

If you want to utilize the benefits of EGL (a faster, cheaper and well-maintained content process), SMEs must be responsible for writing and maintaining the content. The steps would be as follows:

1 Instructional designers conduct research. They define the audience, learning outcomes and objectives to start designing the course.

2 The instructional designer and the SMEs outline the course. The instructional designer designs and co-authors the course, while the SMEs write the content. Often, the former also does the final editing. Having multiple SMEs involved offers a more diverse perspective. If the SMEs harbour different views, they can resolve these during the content creation process.

3 Different SMEs review the course.

4 The course undergoes a governance process and is then published in the LMS or LXP.

5 The SMEs are responsible for keeping the content updated in line with the business.

Organizations opting for the regulated approach can harness the strengths of EGL without relinquishing control or drastically altering their existing procedures. The instructional designer's active role and thorough reviews ensure the content's quality is maintained and standard quality control measures are applied.

CASE STUDY

The need for faster development and higher quality

One of the world's leading logistics firms faced two challenges. One, its central learning teams took too long to create content. Two, the content created by the local learning teams wasn't of high enough quality. Additionally, the central learning team didn't have the capacity to provide any support to the local teams. The resulting lengthy development time hindered the company's ability to train teams at the speed of business.

The company adopted a regulated EGL approach. This not only streamlined content creation and governance but also integrated seamlessly into the existing learning technology ecosystem. It significantly reduced the time to market for training content from the major learning teams while enhancing the quality of material produced by local teams. Through EGL, all teams were empowered to generate learning content more efficiently. In all, they crafted close to 600 courses, with employees worldwide actively contributing to content creation. EGL emerged as the firm's go-to solution for e-learning, allowing employees to create content that previously might have been sidelined due to capacity constraints. Furthermore, SMEs played a pivotal role in hastening and fine-tuning the content creation process within the central learning team.

Understanding whether regulated EGL is the right approach

GOAL AND FOCUS

If your primary aim is to refine the creation process of formal training and maintain control over this process, the regulated approach should be your top choice. This approach addresses the common challenges of slow, large-scale content creation, often for mandatory learning content.

ROLES

The instructional designer enlists SMEs to develop and update the content. The L&D team manages all other facets.

CONTENT CREATION AND MAINTENANCE

While SMEs are tasked with creating and updating content, instructional designers offer guidance and outline expectations. They design the course, brief SMEs and delegate the writing and upkeep to the SMEs.

ACCOUNTABILITY

The emphasis is on supporting formal training procedures, guaranteeing content excellence and ensuring its relevance. The conventional roles of instructional designers and SMEs are preserved, with the L&D department overseeing quality assurance, governance and content release.

CULTURE

An organization marked by a formal, hierarchical structure, with significant separation between operational staff and upper management, is likely best suited for the regulated approach.

Democratized EGL

In the democratized approach to EGL, the emphasis is on sharing knowledge and experience. SMEs eager to contribute are invited to share their expertise, determining the content, format and upkeep of the learning material. This material can range from full courses to microlearning modules and everything in between.

This strategy embodies a decentralized approach to content creation and is defined by a culture of active engagement and collaboration. It uses technology platforms that streamline content production and champions knowledge sharing throughout the organization. As a result, it nurtures a sense of ownership over content and specific areas of expertise. Such a system places value on diverse perspectives, thereby boosting overall employee engagement.

Throughout every stage of EGL implementation, organizations that embrace this democratized strategy proactively promote employee involvement and adaptability. This nurtures a culture of learning and knowledge exchange, making it especially advantageous for organizations that prioritize agility, innovation and employee-driven learning opportunities.

The objective of these knowledge-sharing endeavours is to consolidate all corporate knowledge in a single repository, creating a corporate brain. The goal is for other employees to use this content in their moments of learning need while they are working.

Managed democratized EGL

Very large enterprises rarely adopt a fully regulated approach as traditionally defined. The L&D manager of a large food company told us that the L&D teams typically own only about 5 per cent of content creation, primarily in areas like company-wide compliance courses. The remaining 95 per cent are initiated and completed through the democratized approach by various business units. But this doesn't mean they follow a 100 per cent pure democratized approach. Instead, they build upon the democratized approach's foundation, letting SMEs take the lead in creating learning content and only facilitating this process without assuming control.

How does the managed democratic approach differ from the unregulated democratic approach? The latter involves minimal L&D involvement, granting complete autonomy to course creators with no predefined content creation conditions. We've observed that organizations embracing the fully democratized approach sometimes encounter challenges because clear ownership of the entire EGL initiative is lacking. This can leave authors feeling unsupported, with no defined promotion for EGL concepts and resources. In such cases, EGL creator tools are often viewed as advanced versions of PowerPoint, leading to limited initiative growth.

The managed democratic approach retains the author's responsibility for content creation and topic selection while still providing support and streamlining the process. It enhances the likelihood of EGL initiatives succeeding and facilitates knowledge sharing within the organization. L&D's supporting activities can include promoting the approach, granting access to the content creation platform, creating templates, providing examples and resources, fostering collaboration among SMEs, sending reminders to course creators for updates and efficiently onboarding new SMEs while offboarding departing staff. Thanks to this facilitation, the managed EGL model is often more mature and successful than the completely unregulated democratic approach.

When SMEs gain access to the authoring platform, they receive a framework and resources to ensure a proper start for implementing their ideas and creating courses. These resources are developed and maintained by either the L&D team or a dedicated business unit, such as an enablement department. Some organizations have a central L&D team, while others rely on a network of decentralized training teams. In both cases, these teams are responsible for facilitating and managing the prerequisites for EGL. They ensure continuity by transferring courses to another SME when the original creator leaves the organization, monitor for copyright violations and assist authors in publishing their courses on the LMS or LXP. In certain situations, L&D may also assess courses to ensure quality.

With managed democratized EGL, the L&D department doesn't step back. On the contrary, we see an active role for L&D in some of the most successful EGL implementations.

CASE STUDY
Stronger together: a blend of regulated and democratized EGL

In a case study of a large telecommunications company, we see a great illustration of how the regulated and democratized approaches can go hand in hand, reinforcing one another. The L&D department took the lead in creating and designing the planned formal courses, but they got SMEs to do the actual writing. The courses were published in their LMS and presented as corporate-approved learning modules. This was the regulated approach.

They also implemented a democratized process where SMEs created learning content without any involvement from L&D. They published this content on their intranet and labelled it as EGL content. This label meant that this was created by co-workers sharing their insights and ideas. It wasn't officially approved corporate content and learners couldn't assume that it was 100 per cent correct. They had to vet critical information rather than accepting it at face value. They also made it very clear who created the content, indicating the name and contact information of the course author. This visibility not only improved content quality – given the hesitance to associate one's name with subpar content – it also acknowledged and credited high-quality contributions, positioning the SMEs as domain experts.

The company's strategy didn't end there. When the L&D team set out to design a new course, their first action was checking the intranet's SME-generated content. Should they find pre-existing content on the subject, it would serve as the foundation for the official course. Subsequently, the L&D department would collaborate with the SMEs to refine the content, ensuring it met corporate standards. This upgraded version would then be launched on the LMS. Notably, developing an official course based on SME-contributed content was markedly quicker than the conventional process.

As luck would have it, while they were in the middle of implementing EGL, three-quarters of the L&D staff were let go because of budget cuts. Despite this significant blow to their resources, L&D was still able to create learning materials 12 times faster and multiply the number of their learning materials fivefold. In the end, most of the content was created through the democratized approach.

Understanding whether democratized EGL is the right approach

GOAL AND FOCUS

If your primary aim is to cultivate knowledge sharing, enhance performance and harness employee expertise for informal learning, then the democratized approach may be more suitable. It efficiently shares employees' knowledge and experience with their colleagues, focusing on retaining knowledge and improving performance. This approach also offers the flexibility to extend beyond formal learning, incorporating microlearning formats such as how-to guides, best practices and frequently asked questions.

ROLES

Here, the SME is proactive and assumes the leading role. In a 100 per cent democratized approach, the role of L&D is minimized and the process is not actively facilitated. In a managed democratized approach, L&D's role is to facilitate the overall process, offering tools, guidance and if needed assisting with content creation and distribution.

CONTENT CREATION AND MAINTENANCE

SMEs take charge of both the creation and the upkeep of content, often also dictating the structure and decisions around publishing.

ACCOUNTABILITY

SMEs have complete authority over content creation, ensuring their expertise is accurately conveyed. The approach promotes active employee participation and endorses individual ownership of knowledge-sharing endeavours.

CULTURE

An informal, flat organization with minimal separation between operational personnel and upper management is the type of organization that chooses a fully democratic approach more often than others. Organizations with more hierarchy (almost by definition the larger organizations) tend to find the democratized approach most fitting.

Company and culture

It's been our observation that many organizations underestimate the impact of culture on initiatives like EGL. While a good number of organizations account for variations across locations, only a handful are actively working on bridging the cultural differences between employees. Grasping these cultural nuances and understanding the impact EGL can have on your organization's culture is very important. This is why we want to dive deeper into the culture aspect.

Your company culture has a big role in deciding which EGL approach – regulated or democratized – will best suit your company. EGL, in its turn, will also have a big influence on your company culture. Democratized EGL, in particular, can catalyze a significant shift in your company culture, fostering a learning environment where knowledge acquisition and sharing are highly valued and rewarded. And while *company culture* certainly plays a significant role, so does the *cultural background* of your employees.

Even if organizations present themselves as unified entities, the local cultures can vary across offices and countries. Despite belonging to the same organization, local customs will invariably influence the company culture. Consequently, operations in your Tokyo office may differ from those in Sao Paulo, New York or Amsterdam. This means that the learning culture and the preferred approach to EGL might vary not just from office to office but also from country to country. More so if you employ remote workers from different countries or if your offices are diverse, with employees from various cultural backgrounds, it's crucial to recognize the unique cultural perspectives they bring. This consideration is vital.

As a result of these cultural inclinations, one region might gravitate towards the regulated approach while another could be more inclined to adopt the democratized approach.

I (Videhi) have worked in several different countries, each with a unique local culture that impacted how we worked and shared knowledge. A striking example was my experience working at a multinational consulting company. This company operated across the world in more than 700 locations and I noticed a stark contrast in the work culture between the India and the US branches.

In India, we attended various training programmes, even if they didn't directly relate to our jobs. For example, I'm an e-learning expert, but I had to take training on taxes for compliance reasons. It didn't help me improve in the right direction, other than ticking the boxes for mandatory training. We mostly worked separately in our team, coming together only for project meetings and casual chats to clear doubts. Knowledge sharing was mainly encouraged when a senior employee left the company. In the last two weeks before their departure, we had intense in-person and online sessions to transfer and capture knowledge and retain that knowledge for the organization.

This was different from what my colleagues in the US experienced. They had the autonomy to oversee each other's projects. They could choose what they wanted to learn and even work with a colleague on a project they liked. There was much accountability and a sense of security, allowing them to share what they knew freely.

The six-dimension model by Geert Hofstede serves as a helpful guide for understanding the impact of culture on the workings of a company (and, ultimately, how this would affect EGL implementation).[1]

In the model in Figure 6.1, each culture is assigned a score between 0 and 100 on each dimension. When you compare cultures, you'll see variations in scores across the dimensions. The more significant the gap, the more crucial it is to consider these differences.

Let's dive into the dimensions.

POWER DISTANCE INDEX

This dimension reflects how power is distributed within a culture and how people navigate disparities in power. Societies with high scores typically have more hierarchical structures, with a significant power gap between the privileged and the less privileged. In contrast, low-score societies will strive for equal power distribution and smaller power gaps.

How it affects EGL: In cultures with a significant power distance, empowering employees and adopting a democratized approach may prove challenging or even unfeasible. However, EGL can also be strategically leveraged to transform such cultures and diminish these power differentials.

FIGURE 6.1 Hofstede's 6 Dimension of Culture

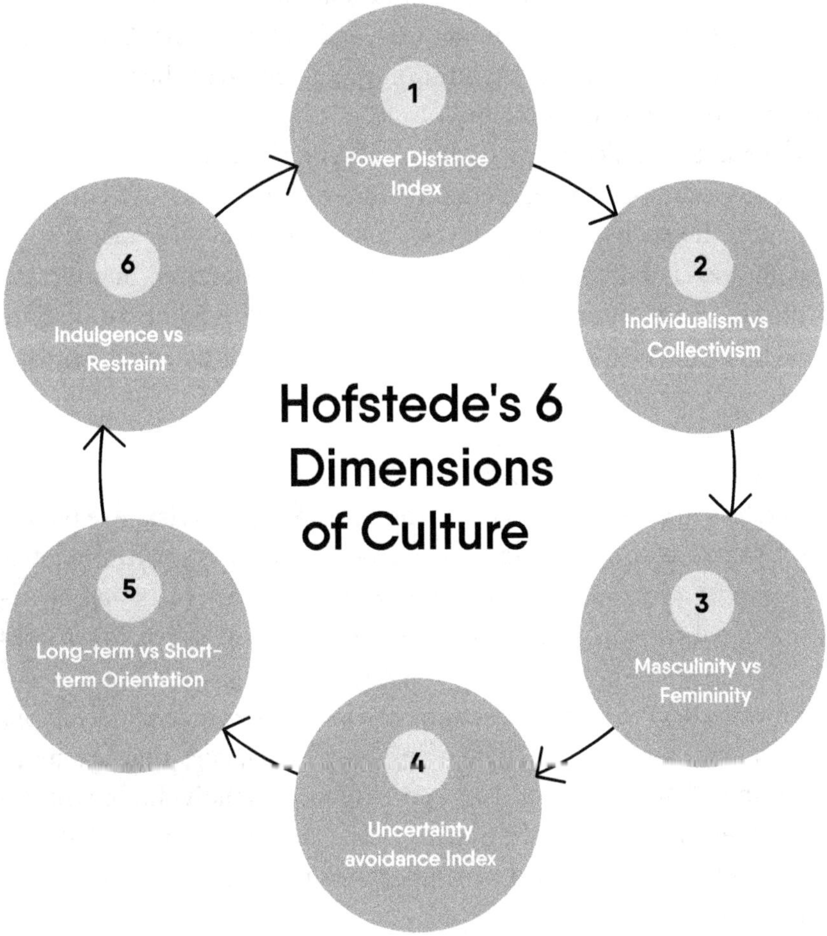

INDIVIDUALISM VERSUS COLLECTIVISM

This dimension measures whether individuals prioritize their personal goals and accomplishments or value the objectives and achievements of the broader society or group more.

How it affects EGL: This factor plays a pivotal role in determining how to foster collaboration among your content authors and the methods of recognizing and rewarding their contributions.

MASCULINITY VERSUS FEMININITY

Cultures tilting towards the 'masculine' end of this spectrum typically emphasize assertiveness, competition and achievement. Conversely, cultures with a 'feminine' orientation prioritize values like nurturing, compassion and overall quality of life.

How it affects EGL: Based on our observation, in cultures that are more masculine-oriented, there often arises the question, 'What's in it for me?' In such settings, introducing incentives like recognition becomes essential to engage and motivate contributors. In contrast, in more feminine-dominated cultures, individuals might readily share their knowledge and insights without anticipating personal benefits, driven by a sense of collective wellbeing.

UNCERTAINTY AVOIDANCE INDEX

This refers to a society's tolerance for uncertainty and risk. Are people comfortable with uncertainty or do they want to avoid it? Societies with high scores on this dimension will have strict rules and structures to make things more predictable, while societies with low scores are more open to change and ambiguity.

How it affects EGL: Taking initiative in societies that heavily avoid uncertainty can be more challenging than in societies that are more accepting of the unknown. This can influence an individual's willingness to engage in your initiative. You can remove a part of this uncertainty by collecting full support from the direct managers of the SMEs.

LONG-TERM ORIENTATION VERSUS SHORT-TERM ORIENTATION

Cultures with a long-term orientation value perseverance and greatly appreciate and respect traditions. In contrast, cultures with a short-term orientation prioritize immediate gratification and adaptability to changing circumstances.

How it affects EGL: Creating content and sharing knowledge are long-term endeavours showing commitment to the organization and its goals. Rewards might not be instantly apparent but can manifest over time. Consequently, EGL implementation and participation are potentially smoother in cultures with a long-term orientation than in those with a short-term focus.

INDULGENCE VERSUS RESTRAINT

Cultures leaning towards indulgence prioritize personal joy and freedom. In contrast, cultures inclined towards restraint enforce more rigid social norms, placing restrictions on immediate gratification.

How it affects EGL: The impact of this dimension on EGL is less significant. Some argue that sharing knowledge and experiences embodies personal freedom, potentially influencing collaborative dynamics. But we haven't observed any notable impact that came from this.

The Hofstede Insights website offers a country comparison tool where users can input different countries and compare their cultural differences. This tool can be useful in refining your EGL strategies with these cultural differences in mind.

CASE STUDY
Creating customer- and location-specific learning content

A global food service company has thousands of customers worldwide, each with multiple locations and distinct requirements. The company has a set of central rules, regulations and guidelines, but it must customize everything to align with each customer's unique specifications. In most cases, even separate locations of a single customer require different rules and guidelines.

The learning department struggled to adapt educational content for every customer's unique needs due to limited resources and lack of detailed knowledge about each customer's policies. This specialized understanding was held by teams directly interacting with the customers at their specific locations.

They used an EGL approach. They gave the site managers and their teams the responsibility and the facilities to create and maintain the specific on-site training and learning content. As a result of using this EGL approach, regional and customer teams have been able to build learning modules 22 times faster than used to be the case with central development and it turns out to be 42 times cheaper as well.

Most companies embarking on EGL typically opt for one of the approaches initially. After a successful first implementation, they explore other methods too, since they now have both content managed by the L&D department and by SMEs. All companies in the long run need a blend of regulated (and owned by L&D) and democratized, managed or not, that is owned by SMEs. However, there are also clients, like the telecommunications company you learned about in the case study, that adopt both methods simultaneously, the managed democratized approach. While feasible, it's crucial to understand that this requires distinct processes. To manage this dual approach effectively, many companies allocate separate L&D staff members to each process, allowing them to concentrate solely on one. This is also good advice to follow if you start with one approach and add another later on – have separate people work on these separate approaches.

Note

1 Hofstede, G (2001) *Culture's Consequences: Comparing values, behaviors, institutions and organizations across nations*, Thousand Oaks, CA: Sage Publications.

7

Potential pitfalls and objections

Implementing Employee-generated Learning isn't as simple as turning on a switch. It doesn't yield results immediately; it's a process that evolves over time, requiring careful attention and ongoing effort. Indeed, EGL implementation is a transformative process and any change invariably encounters some level of resistance. But this resistance isn't inherently negative. In fact, you often need such pushback to effect meaningful change, as it's a fundamental principle of change management. A lack of resistance typically indicates that the proposed change isn't impactful enough to garner attention. If people don't care, they don't respond. This chapter will delve into these potential challenges and counterarguments, providing insights and guidance to help you manoeuvre through these obstacles.

Getting buy-in from leadership and management

Without support from leadership and management, the implementation of EGL becomes a struggle. This initiative requires employees, primarily valued for their unique expertise, to assume an extra responsibility: sharing their knowledge. This is not what they were hired for. For EGL to succeed, you need management support and encouragement. Without it, the EGL initiative might quickly reach a dead end.

Possible solutions

- Initiate informative sessions with management early on. Clarify the advantages of EGL for both them and their departments to ensure their support.

- For buy-in, start at the highest organizational levels and work your way down. This top-down approach is often more effective than the reverse.

- Once you've achieved their support, maintain consistent communication. Provide regular updates and demonstrate tangible results.

- If you face notable resistance from certain managers, consider starting with more open teams. Create success stories within those teams, then use those successes as persuasive examples for the hesitant managers later on.

Uncertainties from subject matter experts

Leadership buy-in doesn't automatically address employees' apprehension about knowledge sharing. SMEs aren't trained educators and they might see the new expectation to teach colleagues as an additional responsibility. Through a survey with SMEs, we gained critical insights into their objections on knowledge sharing:

- Concerns about not get credit for their efforts.
- Absence of incentives or rewards for sharing knowledge.
- No time availability for non-priority initiatives.
- Uncertainty about the value of their content.
- Concerns about their expertise being diminished if everyone has their knowledge.

Not getting credit

Based on our survey, the main reason SMEs are unwilling to partake in knowledge sharing is because they don't believe they will get credit for their work. In some instances, they even believe that others will claim their credit.

POSSIBLE SOLUTIONS

- Clearly identify the content authors to recognize and validate the expertise of the SME.
- Provide assurance to SMEs by explaining how they will receive credit and explain the acknowledgement process.

Absence of incentives or rewards

The SMEs do not see any incentives or rewards for sharing their knowledge.

POSSIBLE SOLUTIONS

- Again, ensure that content authors are clearly recognized, which validates and acknowledges the SME's expertise.
- Consider introducing a reward system specific to knowledge sharing. Incorporating knowledge-sharing contributions into yearly evaluations might offer long-term incentives.
- Include knowledge-sharing tasks in job descriptions, emphasizing that sharing expertise is an inherent part of roles, especially for those with more experience.
- The buy-in of the direct managers is crucial. A manager who encourages knowledge sharing can significantly boost the initiative.
- Encourage managers to participate in content creation. Their involvement can set a positive precedent, demonstrating a commitment to the initiative from leadership.

Low-priority task

If knowledge sharing isn't prioritized, it means there's a lack of support from the direct manager. Thus, it's seen as a supplementary task and not integrated into routine work and responsibilities.

POSSIBLE SOLUTIONS

- Address the concern with direct managers, as their buy-in is vital to rebrand EGL and knowledge sharing as a high-priority initiative.
- Identify and collaborate with managers who are passionate advocates for EGL. Their enthusiasm can be contagious and they can persuade their peers about the importance of EGL.

No time availability

SMEs often express concerns about the time required for content creation for EGL. However, it's crucial to consider the broader context. SMEs are the go-to experts being interviewed when a new course is developed. Since they're the experts in the subjects on which the courses are created, they're often called upon during onboarding sessions and frequently asked to address questions from their peers.

POSSIBLE SOLUTIONS

- Illustrate how investing time in content creation can eliminate repetitive explanations and training sessions. Point out the long-term time savings associated with creating a learning resource.
- Collaborate with SMEs who are already being consulted for their expertise. Since they're already dedicating time to provide input, turning those insights into content may demand only a little more time.
- Making knowledge sharing and content creation part of the job description and a factor in the yearly evaluation is a game-changer. (As is the manager's support.)
- Above all, prioritize effortless processes. Whether it's about creation, tooling, co-authoring, reviewing or publishing, ensure that the fusion of streamlined processes and intuitive tools seamlessly integrates into SMEs' daily routine.

Uncertainty about providing value

Some SMEs indicated that they second-guess whether the content they create would provide value to others. This is an interesting objection and very often indicates that you are on to something great.

Based on our experiences, SMEs who doubt their own knowledgeability very often turn out to be the greatest content creators because they're willing to discuss their point of view and collaborate with other SMEs.

POSSIBLE SOLUTIONS

- Collaborate with the SME to draft a small piece of content, either a short course or a microlearning resource like a how-to guide or checklist.

- Solicit feedback from potential learners or other SMEs to demonstrate its value.

Jeopardizing their position

Several SMEs indicated a concern that by sharing their specialized knowledge, they risk reducing their unique value to the organization – and view this expertise as their 'edge' or competitive advantage.

POSSIBLE SOLUTIONS

- Convince the SME that sharing knowledge is the best way to get recognition as an expert. Moreover, highlight that this sharing also adds to the organization's collective intelligence, which is a valued contribution.

- Foster an environment of transparency and accountability, ensuring psychological safety for the SME. This atmosphere allows them to share without fearing competition.

- Recognizing the SME's contributions is vital. Consider incorporating their efforts into the annual key result areas (KRAs), managed by the HR department. Ultimately, the aim is to seamlessly instil a culture of openness across both team and organizational tiers.

Limitations of subject matter experts

Some of the objections against EGL are based on the fact that SMEs don't have a didactical or e-learning background and therefore cannot create proper learning content. Let's review these objections and see how you can overcome them.

Inexperience with creating assessments

There's a common argument against allowing SMEs to design quizzes and assessments due to their perceived lack of expertise in evaluation. However, our research emphasizes the importance of high-quality assessments with well-constructed questions for formal courses. And often SMEs play a pivotal role in this. We must remember that SMEs possess an in-depth understanding of crucial job elements. Thus, having L&D teams creating vague quizzes is far from sufficient; collaboration with SMEs is key.

In a mid-sized software firm in India, an SME took charge of technical training sessions. In contrast, L&D handled post-training evaluations and mid-year reviews. Despite the high-quality training, L&D found that employees consistently underperformed in the tests. An examination of the assessment questions uncovered their generic and theoretical nature. They resembled textbook questions, devoid of real-world applicability, leading to confusion among trainees. Recognizing this, management fused the SME's technical expertise with L&D's assessment skills. This enriched both the training content and the relevance of the assessments.

When creating a course with the help of an instructional designer, it's usually best for the instructional designer to lead in making the assessments, using input from the SMEs. These tests help check a learner's understanding and let L&D know when someone has finished the course. But with EGL, it's less about checking off course completion and more about sharing knowledge, so detailed tracking isn't as critical.

However, the role of these assessments can change when courses are made through a democratized approach. When courses are optional, the aim of questions isn't so much to test but to teach. They help learners dive deeper into the material on their own and check their understanding without any pressure. Essentially, these questions become tools for self-reflection rather than examination. Modern tools often allow analysis of learner-provided answers, helping authors identify questions that need improvement based on learner feedback. This kind of feedback helps make the EGL content better and more effective over time.

POSSIBLE SOLUTIONS

- For formal top-down courses, creating assessments should be the responsibility of the instructional designer.

- In bottom-up created courses where the SME is responsible for the entire content, including the assessments, choosing and leveraging the right tools can be a viable solution. Selecting an authoring tool that has didactic and analytic capabilities can help you identify the effectiveness of your assessments.

- Organize workshops for your SME authors on how to create effective assessments for e-learning.

Biased learning content

There's a notion that SMEs might have strong attachments to their own perspectives, potentially leading to biased learning content. This challenge isn't exclusive to EGL; even when SMEs relay information to an instructional designer for course creation, that designer must sift through biases to extract objective data. EGL addresses this subjectivity through collaboration.

POSSIBLE SOLUTIONS

- Promote collaboration among diverse SMEs with varied pers-pectives and experiences during content creation. By reconciling their methods, they can collectively identify the best or most balanced approach more efficiently than an instructional designer alone. The result is more comprehensive and varied learning content.

- Implement course reviews by SMEs who weren't part of the original authoring process.

Lack of motivation

Lack of motivation among SMEs to create content is a known hurdle. And not *all* SMEs are expected to be content creators – the influx of content would be overwhelming. So, in some cases, this lack of motivation can be beneficial in preventing the production of unneeded content. As one of our clients noted, '**The best remedy to avoid unnecessary content creation is to assign ownership to SMEs because they don't necessarily want to spend their time there and will only create when they deem it necessary.**'

In our research, we observed an alternative application of the 70:20:10 rule. Roughly 10 per cent of employees in a typical organization are actively willing to share their knowledge. Around 20 per cent are amenable to sharing knowledge if solicited and a significant 70 per cent prefer only to consume knowledge. We label these groups as *The Willing*, *The Able* and *The Lazy*, respectively.

These numbers may vary, but a small percentage – *The Willing* – will voluntarily share their expertise. *The Able* can be convinced to participate but usually won't take the initiative and *The Lazy* will mostly consume content.

POSSIBLE SOLUTIONS

- Identify The Willing, The Able and The Lazy in your organization. The Willing should be your target audience for becoming a content creator. Then, involve The Able as much as you can. Refrain from trying to involve The Lazy.

- Reward and recognition systems can greatly boost and maintain motivation. Rewards don't always equate to financial incentives (even though in some instances knowledge-sharing contributions can be considered during performance evaluations, as mentioned previously). More often than not, recognition serves as a powerful motivator. For instance, when SMEs craft a well-received course or job aid, praise from their colleagues boosts their reputation as an expert. This acknowledgement is a profound motivational factor for many SMEs. We often refer to this effect as 'You get what you reward'. It's essential to think outside the box when recognizing their efforts. Something as straightforward as inviting the SME to discuss their topic with upper management can be deeply impactful.

Lack of applicability of learning content

SMEs often make courses that contain a lot of information. With that the essential bits can sometimes get buried, especially in longer courses with many modules.

Why do they do this? It's because they're used to a history of education where they were given lots of material to study, even if it wasn't directly related to their actual job. Teachers and L&D professionals didn't always consider the context and real needs of the learners, resulting in courses that had too much content.

So, SMEs continue this trend when asked to create content. That's why it's important, with EGL available, to change their focus from just 'content' to the actual 'context' of the job. They should create content that's specific and relevant to the job at hand.

POSSIBLE SOLUTIONS
- Shift the SMEs' focus from content to *context*.
- Offer SMEs a framework for application-oriented learning that facilitates real-world application. The quicker learners can put what they've learned into practice, the more immediate the outcomes become. This direct connection between content and task enriches the learning experience, making it more relevant and impactful.
- We developed a simple yet effective technique for guiding SMEs in creating practical content: the goals-questions-content technique. First, they should define the audience and the goals of the course. Next, they should write down questions that would verify whether

a learner has met these goals. Finally, they should *only* create content that would help the learners answer the questions.

- Promote the creation of microlearning and performance support content. This is by definition shorter, more actionable content that often creates much practical value.

Consider a scenario where a broadband technician is repairing your Wi-Fi router. Would you want them to rely on an outdated online course or would you prefer them to turn to current information and real-time troubleshooting techniques? The technician's efficacy in resolving the problem hinges more on practical experience and immediate assistance than on pre-set training materials. Every troubleshooting scenario presents its own challenges and a generic training course may not address every potential issue. The technician might instead consult the company's mobile app for a quick reference or seek advice from colleagues in real time.

This kind of real-time, practical assistance is what we term *performance support*. Ideally, the content for these situations is crafted by peers who have faced similar challenges or have relevant expertise. The primary focus here is to offer succinct, actionable guidance for technical resolutions or the application of specific skills. The end goal isn't merely to absorb theoretical knowledge or ace a test but rather to provide instantaneous solutions and assistance. The objective is not to memorize theoretical knowledge or pass a test but to deliver immediate solutions and support.

Ensuring quality in EGL materials

When discussing quality in learning content, we need to distinguish two dimensions. First, there's the accuracy of the content itself: is it correct, up to date and factual? Second, there's the didactic quality: is the course structured in a way that facilitates knowledge transfer and application in the best possible way? Before we dive into the details of quality, we want to point out that, with EGL, the simple rule of 'good is good enough' applies.

When creating, reviewing and assessing learning materials, it's essential to ask what level of quality is required. Does it have to be pixel-perfect, top-of-the-class content or is good content *good enough*? In most cases, good content suffices. The question isn't about the polished design, the aesthetic appeal or the level of inter-activity and engagement the content offers. Instead, it's about whether the learning material is effective. Will it enable learners to achieve their goals?

Consider the evolution of video content. In the days before digital cameras and smartphones, integrating video into e-learning was costly, often requiring a full crew, actors and detailed scripts. Today, the narrative has shifted. People can record videos right at their desks using their phones and instantly share with peers. Often, this level of quality is good enough. Our changing perception of quality is influenced by our exposure to less polished content on platforms like YouTube and other social media channels. These may not meet professional standards, but they effectively serve their purpose, which is the most important aspect. As long as the content provides the necessary information and aids learners in their goals, the aesthetic quality or level of polish isn't a crucial factor. What truly counts is the content's relevance and practicality.

Content quality

The best way to improve the quality of content is to have SMEs, not instructional designers, create your learning content. And preferably not one SME but a small group of SMEs – nothing is more effective than this.

CREATING ACCOUNTABILITY

Accountability is a powerful tool for ensuring quality in the content created. One effective strategy to maintain this quality is by making it clear who the author or authors of each course are. Associating the authors' names and contact information with the course serves two main purposes. First, it offers recognition to the SMEs. Acknowledging their expertise and their role in creating the course gives them a sense of ownership and pride, which can increase their engagement and motivate them to contribute more valuable content. Second, having their name attached to the content can drive SMEs to produce high-quality material. After all, no one wants their name linked with poorly crafted content. **The desire to uphold their reputation and be seen as reliable experts in their field encourages SMEs to thoroughly review and refine their content before sharing it with their peers.** Personal accountability can serve as a powerful motivator to ensure the production of high-quality, effective learning materials. The content is a learning tool for the other employees and a reflection of the expertise and dedication of the SMEs who create it.

Building an effective feedback mechanism

Many learning systems give learners the capability to rate content, for example on a scale of one to five stars. Such ratings are not just crucial for guiding other learners, they also ensure lower-rated content doesn't frequently appear in searches. But this feedback mechanism can be taken a step further by allowing learners to comment on the content directly. They can pinpoint missing or incorrect parts, provide alternative solutions or suggest improvements. This type of feedback can be invaluable for authors looking to refine their content. However, it's essential to foster an environment where this feedback is given in a constructive and respectful manner.

POSSIBLE SOLUTIONS

- Have SMEs, not instructional designers, create the content.
- Preferably get a small group of SMEs to collaborate on creating a course.
- Make sure all courses are reviewed by other SMEs.
- Make sure the SME is not only responsible for creating the content but also feels responsible for keeping that course content up to date – make them accountable.
- Ensure there is a feedback option for learners to comment on the learning content and that this feedback is given directly to the course authors.

Didactical quality

A potential drawback often cited in relation to EGL is the quality, or lack thereof, of the content. What if SMEs, despite their expertise, create sub-par content? There are strategies to prevent this. Instructional designers can offer guidance and tool vendors can ensure their tools are conducive to creating quality content. We've even incorporated instructional design knowledge into our tools, partly drawing from a database of design rules and partly utilizing AI. Interestingly, based on our customer feedback, EGL content often surpasses that created by professional instructional designers.

The discussion on the quality of EGL content brings up two key considerations: the accuracy and relevance of the content and its didactic quality. When it comes to the former, SMEs, given their in-depth knowledge in their field, are arguably better equipped to produce accurate and up-to-date content. This is one of the core reasons behind the advocacy for EGL. Therefore, when we talk about a potential lack of quality in EGL materials, the focus generally lies on the didactic quality: is the content well structured and engaging or is it poorly written and devoid of interactivity? A potential shortfall of EGL could be that while SMEs are experts in their fields, they might not have the necessary skills to present information in an educationally sound manner.

Poor didactic quality can suggest a lack of organization, clear language, appropriate formatting or a combination. These issues pertain to the essentials needed to transform a piece of information into useful, learnable knowledge. It's true that SMEs, as experts in their *own* fields, are typically not trained in the art of crafting high-quality learning materials, nor are they necessarily interested in immersing themselves in learning theory.

But a learning manager once told us that it's easier to teach an SME how to design effective e-learning content than to train an instructional designer on comprehensive business knowledge and insights. It's very likely that this is true. In the context of learning on the job, what matters most is how actionable and applicable the content is rather than how interactive it is. Employees look for practical knowledge that they can immediately utilize in their work. As a result, the focus should be less on embellishing the content with interactivity and more on the content itself. Interactivity is typically used as a tool for practice and recall, an approach more familiar to the realm of L&D than to the domain of the SME. The emphasis should always be on providing clear, concise and practical information that meets the learner's immediate needs.

To aid SMEs in generating effective content, presenting examples and templates within the content-authoring tool can be beneficial. A fully fleshed-out course can act as a prototype, guiding SMEs towards their final objective and highlighting optimal practices in content design and organization. Templates can be even more effective. Templates are pre-structured guides that can be filled out to create content or a course on a specific topic. (To give you a better understanding, some examples of course templates we have in our authoring tool are Salesforce Training, Social Media Strategy, Basics of User Research and Fundamentals of Project Management.) Templates reduce the cognitive load on SMEs by providing a predetermined structure, allowing them to focus on inputting their expertise into the predetermined spaces. They don't have to worry about the content's structure or design. Having these templates directly available in the course authoring tool makes the process even easier. SMEs can log in and use a template as a starting point for content creation. The easier it is for SMEs to access and use these tools, the more likely they are to create learning materials.

POSSIBLE SOLUTIONS

- Encourage SMEs to use the goals-questions-content technique or a do-know framework to structure and steer their thoughts towards actionable content. (We'll explain this further in Chapter 10.)

- Encourage SMEs to create performance support content instead of courses.

- Train SMEs in creating better learning content. It's more effective to teach them how to create proper courses than to correct each course.

- Provide example courses or templates.

- Create a checklist for creating courses. This can include standards on content, images, questions and accessibility among others.
- Build an internal online community where SMEs can ask questions, share insights and support each other.
- Hold an onboarding process for SMEs for course creation, teaching them how to use the tools, best practices and so on.
- Set up a help desk that SMEs can turn to when needed.

AI-ASSISTED CREATOR TOOLS

From the start, we knew we had to address this potential quality objection towards Employee-generated Learning. If the quality of the content is insufficient, the whole idea of EGL will not work. If the quality serves its purpose but is perceived as inadequate by L&D professionals, it could be a barrier to success.

We knew that with Easygenerator, we had to offer didactical, instructional design and writing support. We started out by embedding live support into the tool, delivered by our incredible support team. And the support they offer is not limited to questions about the software; we also offer didactical support. This support goes beyond just software-related queries; we also provide didactical assistance. Our team can aid authors in designing a course or review a course on their behalf. Whatever it takes to ensure the SME produces good-quality e-learning content. We even made this our brand promise: 'With Easygenerator, you can share your knowledge. Easygenerator is easy to use, we have unprecedented built-in support and you can join onboarding sessions. Despite all of this, if you are struggling to get started, we will schedule a one-on-one session until you are confident you can make it work by yourself.'

Simultaneously, we've been increasing the software-driven support for authors. Right from the start we launched the Learning Objective Maker, a tool designed to help SMEs draft robust learning objectives based on Bloom's taxonomy. We've introduced editing help through Easy AI and automated question generation. And our latest offering is the Outline Builder, a tool that generates an action-oriented, rather than content-centric, course outline from the author's input.

Our vision is to keep expanding this support. The ultimate goal? Integrate a didactical and instructional designer into the software itself. Imagine software that coaches authors based on their actions, directing them towards creating superior content. This solution will combine a rule-based engine and an AI application. **If we succeed at this, it will combine the business knowledge of the SME with the instructional design and didactical knowledge of an instructional designer.**

Although we're certainly progressing in that direction, it's a step-by-step process. In our mind, this software coach will not replace our support team but will complement it. That is our general standpoint on AI as well – we see it as a supportive technology, not one that can replace people. We want people to have the ultimate control.

8

Employee-generated Learning and tooling

Death of the corporate LMS?

The prevailing trends are increasingly shifting the responsibility of learning and personal development towards the worker. Consequently, there's a growing emphasis on bottom-up, learner-initiated education and support. Historically, the learning management system was the primary system in place, geared towards controlling and facilitating top-down learning. I (Kasper) talked about the 'death of the LMS' in a presentation at the DevLearn e-learning conference in Las Vegas in 2013. My perspective was that learning trends were transitioning from a formal, top-down approach to a more informal, bottom-up style. The LMS wasn't designed to cater to this new trend. You can argue that I was a bit ahead of the curve and that *death* was maybe a bit of an overstatement. But it is a fact that the role and prominence of the LMS have been waning over the past decade and this trend continues.

This evolving landscape led to the emergence of new tools. These are platforms designed to focus on learning initiated by the worker when they need it. As a result, LXPs have sometimes been dubbed the 'Netflix of learning', acting as the 'streaming service' for education. As learning and performance content nowadays leans more towards the LXP style, its popularity has surged. This rise of LXPs is beginning to challenge the once-dominant position of LMSs. Some LXPs are even adding features for pushing and monitoring learning to their tools. This is a direct threat to the classic LMS.

For workers or learners, this is a confusing development. It's not always clear where content is housed. Is it in the LMS? The LXP? A performance support system? Or platforms like Yammer or the corporate intranet? And the task of navigating through all these systems to find the right content can be a hassle. Given these challenges, it's our belief that in five years neither the LMS nor the LXP will be the dominant learning system. The modern learner wants a unified platform that offers all learning resources under one roof. With the fast rise of AI, delivering timely answers and content to learners in a streamlined manner is becoming more achievable. AI-driven tools will have a severe impact on how learners access and retrieve knowledge.

From an EGL standpoint, the shift from the LMS is understandable. LMS stands for learning *management* system and management stands for top-down, L&D-controlled learning. However, the trend is moving *away* from control – away from the LMS, so the LXP trend is rising – but the story doesn't end there. To facilitate everything a company needs for learning, development and support, you need a combination of systems, tools and databases. You need a 'learning technology ecosystem'.

The learning technology ecosystem

Later in the chapter we present an overview of some of the components of a potential learning technology ecosystem. The flow will vary for every company; what we provide is a general idea. In this book we only want to highlight the main components and explain the developments connected to them. In this chapter we also share what you should consider when building your learning technology ecosystem, together with our recommendations for choosing the right tools.

Authoring tools

Authoring tools, also known as creator tools, are essential for crafting learning and support materials. Among these tools, instructional design authoring ones stand out. They are complex and tailored for instructional designers to create sophisticated e-learning modules. Often, these modules address mandatory content like compliance and security training.

Conversely, there are SME authoring tools designed for simplicity. They come with a gentle learning curve, considering these users often have roles beyond content creation. These tools are fundamental in the Employee-generated Learning process. Organizations should choose their authoring tools with care to ensure they integrate well with their learning technology ecosystem. In the subsequent section of this chapter, we'll go over the key criteria for selecting these tools and methods to assess potential vendors. By understanding these criteria, you'll have a better understanding of how to choose the right tools for supporting effective EGL within your organization.

Learning management systems

The LMS is primarily designed to support L&D in managing their learning initiatives; it doesn't have the learners at its core. With the growing emphasis on knowledge sharing and performance support, it's clear that learners are now expected to take more charge of their workplace development. As such, the popularity and relevance of the LMS are waning.

We mentioned that many LMSs are improving or adding features like their search and learning paths to compete with the upcoming LXPs. Whether that will work remains to be seen. After all, the LMS was designed for admin and management, while LXPs were designed to personalize the learning experience. So, the attempt to change this is similar to trying to convert a truck into a racing car. On top of that, there are many other tools out there that are better for specific tasks, like making learning content. These specialized tools often do their jobs better than a general tool like an LMS. The good news is that it's now easier to connect these tools together and share information between them. We think the future will have many small, specialized tools working together. This is, in fact, one of the main decisions you have to make in building a learning technology ecosystem. Do you want to use a mix of specialized tools or are you looking for one tool or one vendor that can offer almost everything in one go?

The role of the LMS might change. Instead of being the main way people learn at work, it might just be one of many tools. We can see this change happening now. Some LMS companies are buying LXPs and tools for making content to offer more. Meanwhile, some big LXPs are buying LMS systems and content-making tools. After buying them, they connect these tools together and offer them as a package.

Learning experience platforms

LXPs have a different setup than LMSs. Where an LMS is designed to *push* learning towards the learners, the goal of an LXP is to allow the learner to *pull* learning content from it. LMSs are like a television with a set viewing programme; LXPs are like Netflix where you choose what you watch, discover new content and even get recommendations. Some of them also add an element of social learning, as you can find domain experts. They enable social learning through interactions with peers or experts, resembling the way social media networks function. They make recommendations on mentors or buddies who match the learner's skills and learning paths.

While some LXPs lack tracking-and-tracing capabilities – arguing that with bottom-up learning there's no necessity to monitor results from an L&D viewpoint – others do include this feature. This makes them slightly reminiscent of traditional LMS systems.

Despite all their perks, smooth user interfaces and intelligent algorithms, LXPs are not a magic wand that fixes everything about corporate learning. One might even say that they're a glorified version of the LMS. While the LXP offers a more engaging user experience, it frequently recycles the same traditional content with little regard to contextualization. Leading learning professional and Chief Insights Officer at Fosway Group, David Perring, points out: 'LXP is certainly not business smart, or fit for purpose for workflow resources or performance support . . . It's the equivalent of walking into the library and searching for a book when what you wanted was to simply land on the pages you needed.'[1]

This is where AI enters the picture. When you query a search engine such as Google, it provides you with a list of websites where you can find the answer. Similarly, an LMS and an LXP operate by guiding you to a course or other learning material to search for that answer. However, if you've used tools like ChatGPT, you've seen a notable difference. Instead of pointing you to a website, it directly gives you the information or the answer you were seeking. We foresee the same evolution in learning systems. LMS, LXP and PSS (performance support systems) – all the systems that deliver content to the learner or worker – will be significantly influenced by AI solutions. Instead of offering directions, these AI tools will provide immediate answers. We will explore this in greater depth in the final chapter of this book.

One widespread issue we've observed is that after investing in an LXP, companies transfer only a portion of their learning content from the LMS to the LXP. Often, they conclude that just a fraction of the learning material is suitable for the LXP. As a result, they find themselves with an LXP that barely has any content. We've termed this the 'empty LXP syndrome'. A common remedy for this is the acquisition of third-party content. This shortage of content also sometimes serves as a reason for adopting an EGL strategy. Content crafted by SMEs is generally more hands-on and concise than the more extensive courses L&D teams produce, making the SME-created content a natural fit for the LXP.

Performance support systems

Beyond the LMS and the LXP, there's the performance support system. It started out as online assistance for software tools but has evolved considerably over the years. These tools are specifically designed to aid workers during their learning process, leading to their alternative name: 'workflow support tools'. Their primary purpose is to enable employees to address problems and challenges as they arise in their work. By providing them with immediate, practical information tailored to specific learning needs, learners can get back into their workflow as quickly as possible. And this is the direction learning is moving.

However, it's worth noting that the present generation of PSS tools is relatively basic. The key thing with performance support is context. Understanding who the user is, their current task and their location allows for a more refined content selection or even proactive content suggestions before a learner identifies this need. Currently, many PSS tools primarily fetch and display content based on the selection of roles, processes and tasks. Yet there's significant potential here. As PSSs integrate AI, they'll become smarter and more attuned to context. When that happens, it will have a huge impact on corporate learning. The PSS would become the ideal tool to bring all the experiences and knowledge stored in the corporate brain to workers in a quick, convenient and smart way.

A current challenge is the limited compatibility of PSS systems with established industry standards like SCORM and AICC, which makes the integration of PSS into a learning technology ecosystem very challenging.

Results tracking

A learning technology ecosystem is built on its ability to connect components, exchange data and analyse this data. Historically, all learning results were stored inside the LMS. But now, learning occurs everywhere. This gave rise to the LRS (learning record store) – a database designed to capture learning results from various sources, allowing for comprehensive analysis and reporting. This is where standards, like AICC and SCORM, become important.

AICC AND SCORM

AICC and SCORM stand as hallmark e-learning standards, developed to ensure smooth interoperability between various learning systems and content creation tools. They allow for the tracking and tracing of learner outcomes. AICC, which has its roots back in 1988, primarily catered to the aviation industry's niche needs. In contrast, SCORM, created in 2000 by the ADL (a branch of the US Department of Defense), found more general application across multiple sectors.

Both standards allow you to track and trace learning that is happening in an LMS and store these results inside that LMS.[2]

PROJECT TIN CAN, xAPI AND LRS

As we discussed, learning is no longer confined to the LMS. It happens in many places, all at once. So, SCORM and AICC fall short, as they can only monitor and report on learning activities housed within the LMS. Furthermore, content within the LMS is generally trapped, lacking easy export options.

Recognizing this limitation, the ADL, in partnership with the AICC, embarked on a quest to develop a new, more flexible standard. Their mission? To replace both SCORM and AICC with a tool that could track learning activities regardless of where they occurred and store the results in a standalone database. This initiative was named Project Tin Can.[3]

Emerging from this research was the xAPI, introduced to the world in 2013. API stands for application programming interface, a tool that enables different software systems to interact seamlessly. The 'x' in xAPI symbolizes *experience*, underscoring its ability not just to capture traditional learning outcomes but to document myriad learning experiences.

When we compare xAPI with its predecessors, SCORM and AICC, a significant difference stands out: SCORM and AICC are bound to the LMS. They're designed to administer courses and track results but solely within the LMS environment. In contrast, xAPI isn't tied to any one system. A key feature of xAPI is its database, the LRS. This isn't just a database, it's the heart of modern learning technology ecosystems. With learning now dispersed across various tools and platforms, there's a growing need for a centralized repository to gather, store and process this extensive data. Here, xAPI and LRS shine, making it feasible to aggregate and analyse this vast pool of information.

CMI5

xAPI is a broad standard that you can use to capture learning data and learning results from anywhere. cmi5 arises from xAPI. It defines interoperability rules that determine how learning content is launched, imported, authorized and reported in an LMS environment. These rules define how LMS interacts with xAPI-enabled learning content. It's the new SCORM standard based on xAPI.

Despite making SCORM look like a thing of the past, xAPI has its limitations, especially when it comes to determining which content to contain in an LMS. Some advantages of cmi5 are:

- It was designed with modern e-learning in mind – cmi5 is built on xAPI, making it lightweight, efficient and scalable across platforms and devices.
- cmi5 simplifies data tracking compared with SCORM and xAPI, ensuring compatibility between different learning units and LMSs, providing a seamless computer-managed experience.
- Unlike SCORM, cmi5 allows course structures in the LMS while hosting content externally, enabling global access to content through content delivery networks.

Overall, cmi5 brings together the best of SCORM and xAPI, creating a comprehensive specification that acts as a bridge between LRSs and LMSs, offering various advantages. It adds a powerful dimension to your LMS.

Data lakes

A data lake is a central database where data is collected from all over the company. It also comes with data modelling and analysis tools, or it can connect to those tools. It's impossible to upload SCORM results into a data lake; you can only do that with xAPI, which is based on an open data standard called XML.

You can create all kinds of reports from a data lake, but you can also analyse the data. For the first time we can now understand and measure the direct effects of learning programmes on work performance. We already know several companies that have realized this. For instance, a global ICT firm made an unexpected discovery: some of their learning activities were linked to a drop in performance. This wasn't a sign of ineffective training but rather showed *overtraining*. Upon reducing the training intensity, they saw an immediate improvement in performance. Though this might not have been the result they expected, it was a significant breakthrough. It shows that we can now adjust training in real-time based on real results.

L&D has been struggling with proving the value of learning. Sure, there's a common belief that corporate learning is essential, but how do you quantify its impact? Older standards like SCORM and AICC provided basic metrics, such as course completion rates, but they couldn't correlate learning with business performance. This gap meant that showcasing a clear return on investment for learning initiatives was almost impossible. Now, however, you can combine learning data with performance data and analyse the impact of your learning activities.

The flows of a learning technology ecosystem

In a conventional top-down learning flow, as seen in Figure 8.1, it all begins with the HR or L&D department. Courses are crafted by instructional designers using specialized tools, then rolled out to learners through an LMS. While the LMS usually offers courses directly assigned to learners, its search functionality for other courses can be limited. Course outcomes and metrics are then captured either within the LMS itself or in a separate database.

A second, alternative flow is when content is shaped either directly by or in partnership with SMEs. These courses can be driven by either the L&D or the SME. If it's the former, it's typically hosted on the LMS. However, if it leans more towards knowledge sharing, it may find a home elsewhere, perhaps an LXP. If it's microlearning or performance support content, then a performance support system can also be an option. A PSS is software that can quickly present information to the worker while working. In cases where neither an LXP nor a PSS is available, platforms like SharePoint, Teams or Yammer might be used. Some companies use things like Workplace from Facebook or other tools.

FIGURE 8.1 The flows of a learning technology ecosystem

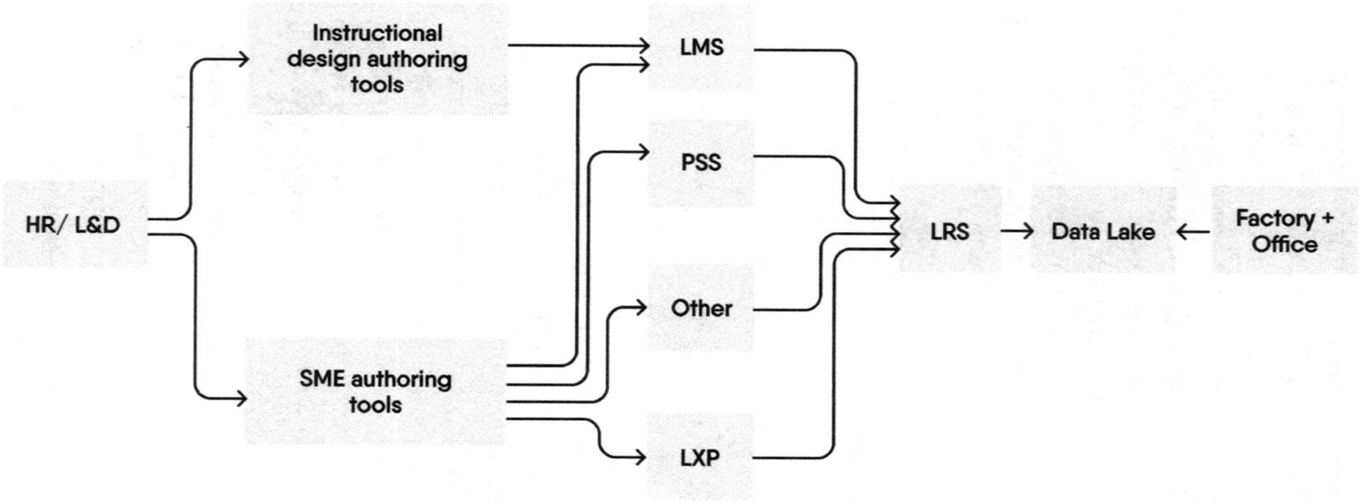

The biggest difference between these flows is where the initiative lies. In the top-down flow, the initiative for both content creation and learning lies with the L&D department. In the bottom-up flow, the initiative for content creation lies with the SME and the initiative for learning with the worker.

Lastly, when we talk about the data part of the learning technology ecosystem, two primary tools come to mind: LXPs and data lakes. LXPs are databases that receive and store learning results from LMSs, LXPs or any xAPI-enabled learning event for that matter. A data lake is a database that can hold and analyse vast amounts of information from different sources. This doesn't refer only to business data, you can also push learning results from an LXP towards a data lake. Consequently, now for the first time you can combine learning content with performance content and quantify the impact of learning on performance.

Key considerations in selecting learning tools

If you're in the market for a learning tool, we've got invaluable pointers for you. Initially, we'll share some universal recommendations relevant to the entire learning technology ecosystem. This applies whether you're aiming to construct a complete learning environment or simply scouting for individual components, such as an LMS or an LXP. Then we'll delve into authoring tools, which have a significant impact on EGL in your processes.

Software-as-a-Service (SaaS) vs on-premise

All software is gradually moving towards the cloud. Some IT departments prefer on-premise solutions for security and control as they're installed on your corporate servers. But cloud-based SaaS is viewed as the future-proof option. Here's a breakdown to ensure you make an informed choice.

SPEED

SaaS is typically ready to use immediately after account creation. In contrast, on-premise solutions can require between days and months for complete setup. If you wanted to run a pilot to explore EGL, SaaS is your best option because you wouldn't have to wait for IT.

MAINTENANCE AND SOFTWARE UPDATES

Software environments are constantly evolving. While on-premise solutions may update once or twice a year (requiring new installations each time), SaaS often receives frequent, seamless updates. An emerging trend in SaaS is continuous deployment, where updates are instantly integrated without disrupting users. This means that you don't have to wait half a year to a year for bug fixes or promised features. When something is ready, it's instantly available for your use.

COST CONSIDERATIONS

The main question here is: will you purchase or get a subscription? When you purchase installed software, you're required to make an upfront payment for the software licence. This initial expense can be quite significant. After this initial investment, a yearly maintenance fee is usually applicable to ensure smooth functioning and receive updates. In contrast, SaaS models predominantly operate on a subscription basis. The immediate cost is less compared with purchasing the software outright. Instead of a large initial sum, you're committed to a periodic fee, often monthly or yearly.

If you analyse the costs in the short run, the first-year expenses for purchased software tend to be heftier due to the initial acquisition cost. Subscription services, meanwhile, are more cost-efficient in the initial stages. But in the long run, purchased software might become more cost-effective because once you've covered the initial purchase cost, you're only left with the lower annual maintenance fees.

There are two more things to take into account. The first is hosting. When you purchase software, you have to host it, meaning you're responsible for the internal servers, IT personnel and any maintenance costs. SaaS offerings are hosted by the service provider. This means no headaches related to server space or maintenance.

The second is licence flexibility. Buying software often means acquiring a set number of licences. If your user base grows, you can buy more licences, but if the user count shrinks, your unused licences become a waste. Conversely, with SaaS solutions you can add and remove users and your fee will be adapted accordingly. You only pay for what you need.

PRIVACY AND SECURITY

Security is vital when selecting software tools, especially when sensitive employee information and proprietary company content will be stored. Your IT department typically has a set protocol to evaluate software security, often using a standardized questionnaire for vendors.

Before getting your IT department involved, one initial step you can take is to request an external security report from the software vendor. Most SaaS companies undergo an annual penetration test. This test, performed by an external entity, attempts to breach the vendor's defences, essentially 'hacking' the system to identify potential vulnerabilities. If a vendor has addressed any discovered issues and can provide a recent external penetration report without any unresolved risks, it's an encouraging sign of their commitment to security. However, if they can't provide a satisfactory report made within the last 12 months, consider it a red flag and don't even involve your IT team; the vendor is already unqualified.

Another crucial consideration is the software's adherence to privacy laws, which can vary significantly depending on where the company's servers are situated and where the users are located. For instance, in the European Union, the General Data Protection Regulation (GDPR) sets the standard. The United States doesn't have a federal equivalent, but some states have stringent regulations, like California's CCPA and Virginia's VCDPA. A vendor should be able to prove that they comply to support both. Just ask for a data protection agreement (DPA). All the rules and regulations regarding privacy are described there in detail. Your legal or IT teams can help review them. If a vendor cannot present a DPA, move on to the next one.

In our view, SaaS and subscription-based software have the edge over on-premise solutions. If a vendor doesn't have an SaaS option, it might indicate that they're not keeping pace with industry standards. Above all, ensure that your selected software upholds the highest levels of security and privacy.

Accessibility

Software must be accessible to individuals with disabilities. Vendors should ensure their software caters to people with visual, auditory or other handicaps. There are laws addressing this. In Europe, the standard is the Web Accessibility Directive and in the US it's the Americans with Disabilities Act. Vendors should comply. One way to check compliance is by asking for a VPAT (Voluntary Product Accessibility Template), which indicates how the software meets accessibility guidelines and where it doesn't. Moreover, few other accessibility evaluation tools can measure a software's accessibility, rating it between 0 and 100 or grading it in levels A, AA, AAA. These evaluation metrics determine the level of conformance with the key accessibility guidelines. If you include audio or video content in a course, you must provide alternative options for learners who can't hear or see well.

Electronic accessibility is evaluated in three levels:

- Level A: This is the minimum level. This requires having audio captions for recorded audio or video content.
- Level AA: On top of Level A requirements, you must have live captions with any live audio or video content.
- Level AAA: On top of Level AA requirements, your recorded audio content should have sign language interpretation.

Supported standards

The dominating standard in our industry still is SCORM and we do not understand why that is. The latest version is SCORM 2004 and yes, that name does indeed indicate that that version was launched in 2004. That was two decades ago – a time when many of us were proud owners of the famous Nokia 7610 or Motorola Razr. This makes SCORM as ancient as these outdated devices. Beyond its age, SCORM can only track, trace and store learner results in an LMS. In contrast, xAPI, introduced in 2013, has been mature for years and offers many significant advantages over SCORM and AICC:

- xAPI is the only way to track and trace learning from any location – SCORM cannot.
- Consequently, xAPI is the only way to create a learning technology ecosystem.
- SCORM is created to track learners' results. In contrast, xAPI can:
  - track learning usage
  - measure completion rates
  - identify where learners face challenges
  - provide data on the quality of questions.
- SCORM restricts learning to your LMS and captures results exclusively within the LMS, preventing data export.
- xAPI avoids vendor lock-in by allowing data extraction from an LMS or external storage in an LRS.
- xAPI is essential for sharing information with non-learning systems (like a data lake).
- Lastly, xAPI courses can be published anywhere. This changed learning content. These xAPI-based courses are developed in HTML5 with tracking capabilities, functioning similarly to mini-websites adaptable to various platforms, including intranets. Many authoring tools offer the feature to publish courses to web servers, from which you can generate a link or embed code. This link or code can be shared across multiple platforms such as Slack, Teams, email, WhatsApp and social media. Essentially, if you can share a YouTube video, you can also distribute this learning material. Importantly, all learning data and results remain securely stored in a centralized database, the LRS.

There is only one conclusion: you should disqualify any learning tool – whether it's an LMS, LXP or authoring tool – that doesn't support xAPI.

One or multiple vendors?

Choosing a single vendor can streamline processes: you have to deal with only one point of contact, ensuring all components of your system work together seamlessly. This not only makes tool management more straightforward but also results in a consistent user experience. On the downside, vendors excel in one aspect of their solution but may fall short in others. For instance, a vendor that offers a top-tier LMS might not necessarily provide the best LXP or authoring tool. Moreover, relying heavily on one vendor can introduce dependency risks. It could reduce your negotiation leverage and even trap you in a vendor lock-in situation. If, for example, you create content within an LMS and store results in that same LMS, exporting that content or those results to another system could become an insurmountable challenge. A case in point is a Dutch university that used Blackboard as their LMS and found themselves tethered to it for a decade due to this vendor lock-in issue. Opting for a best-of-breed approach allows you to select the most fitting tool for each part of your learning technology ecosystem.

Responsiveness

Responsive content automatically adapts to the device and screen size on which it's being viewed. Learners access content through a variety of devices: PCs, laptops, tablets, phones and more, each with its own resolution specifications. Your chosen software must be versatile enough to support all these devices and screen sizes seamlessly. If a software solution fails in this aspect, it's a significant red flag and disqualifier.

Key considerations in selecting authoring tools

While the considerations we've discussed so far are relevant to authoring tools as well, there are additional aspects to bear in mind specifically for these tools, especially within an EGL context.

Types of authoring tools

CLOUD-BASED TOOLS

These are the SaaS tools discussed earlier in this chapter. With simple login credentials, authors can access cloud-based tools to collaborate across different domains and create content quickly. The software is centrally updated and due to cloud storage, authors can create content anytime, anywhere. It is also device agnostic, which means you can use any kind of device for authoring. With SaaS, high-speed internet connectivity is a must-have.

DESKTOP-BASED TOOLS

Installed directly on your desktop, these tools do not align with our general preference for SaaS solutions. This is because desktop-based tools tend to be pricier, feature-rich, highly intricate and come with a steep learning curve. They require trained instructional designers for effective and efficient use. They aren't ideal for SMEs, marking another shortcoming. Authors must store content and media on their desktops, uploading them to courses each time – a potentially lengthy process. Offline training review on the local computer is feasible, yet manual updates are required. The local storage aspect poses a risk of data loss. We don't advise using desktop software for EGL authoring; possibly, only for scenarios where connectivity is an issue.

HYBRID MODELS

The third option is to have a rapid authoring tool incorporated within your LMS or LXP. However, these generally can't rival dedicated authoring tools. Furthermore, your content remains restricted to that system without export capability. Currently in their infancy, these tools are costly and often lack attractive content design and smooth integration.

Overall, our advice is to go for a specialized SaaS authoring solution.

Ease of creation

USER-FRIENDLY INTERFACE

Regardless of your SMEs' technical knowledge or e-learning content creation skills, the tool's intuitiveness is a crucial consideration. A user-friendly interface ensures quick onboarding and motivates consistent content creation by your authors. Prioritizing ease of use means building on existing knowledge, eliminating the need for repetitive content creation. You'll want an authoring tool that offers straightforward features to produce relevant, engaging content without a steep learning curve.

INTERACTIVE FEATURES

Enriching course content with interactive elements can have a significant impact on learner engagement and knowledge retention. Likewise, adding multimedia elements elevates the material's appeal, even helping learners understand concepts better. **What's important here is the ease of creating interactive content.** Easy-to-create interactive blocks will immensely impact SMEs' content creation experience – especially for SMEs who don't have experience with such tools.

MICROLEARNING CONTENT

It's crucial that your authoring software supports not only the creation of comprehensive courses but also of microlearning or performance support content. This includes resources like best practices, how-to guides, frequently asked questions, checklists and more. Such concise pieces of content empower SMEs to easily share their expertise and provide valuable, on-the-job support for colleagues.

INCORPORATING AND EMBEDDING CONTENT

The software you select should be capable of embedding legacy content, supporting a variety of formats, including PowerPoint, Word, PDF, Excel, MP3, .wav and HTML5. This embedding involves preserving the content in its original form. While certain content can be imported into authoring tools and converted into editable content or course pages, the quality can suffer. For example, PowerPoint imports yield better results while Word and PDF files don't. Video embedding is a definite must-have though, particularly to enable content curation.

MULTILINGUAL CAPABILITIES

For organizations operating globally, the ability to offer content in an array of languages is vital. Numerous authoring tools on the market provide translation features. An authoring tool that has an interface compatible with a broader spectrum of languages undoubtedly has a competitive advantage.

Support

CONTENT AND DIDACTICAL SUPPORT

Choose an authoring tool with a built-in support channel. For instance, at Easygenerator our support team is available 24/5 to answer questions about tool usage and even provide didactical assistance. Similarly, some of our competitors, like iSpring, offer strong support at no extra charge. Such support can reduce your workload and play a critical role in the success of your content creators. Immediate in-app guidance and personal onboarding sessions are also crucial to familiarize SMEs with your tool. Moreover, the presence and expertise of a customer success team are vital – they will assist you, the EGL managers and other stakeholders.

TEMPLATES AND RESOURCES

Many authoring tools come with templates and resources that authors can use as a start for their learning content, which is most helpful.

COLLABORATION

Creating content by and with SMEs is something that requires collaboration. Collaboration can happen between L&D professionals and SMEs or among a group of SMEs. Through collaboration, co-authors can create richer content. Tools with co-authoring, reviewing and updating capabilities make the process easier and more manageable. These features also allow authors to solicit feedback from peers or external parties, which accelerates corrections and cuts down revision time. This collaboration aspect is another reason why desktop authoring tools aren't favoured – they lack these communication and collaboration tools.

User management

REVIEW AND GOVERNANCE

Regulated EGL approaches typically involve a review and governance process before content is published. Tools should support content approval workflows, allowing designated individuals or teams to review and approve content before publication. For example, in large enterprises these tools need to support different roles like administrators, reviewers and regular authors. In these companies, there are many teams working on different EGL projects. An administrator needs to manage these teams, organize courses and keep the content in order. In smaller companies, you might only have someone creating content and someone else checking it, but even that is effective for ensuring governance.

ADMIN AND REPORTING FUNCTIONS

Managing your SME accounts is vital. Your authoring tool should offer functionalities to add or remove SMEs. If an account is deleted, there should be an option to transfer that account's courses to another user; an admin panel would support these actions. Reporting tools are another important consideration. Information on author activity and productivity helps oversee the system and also reflects the success of your EGL approach, which is invaluable for everyday management and for reporting to stakeholders.

Publication options

The chosen tool should offer streamlined, flexible publication options. For smooth integration with LMS and LXP systems, authoring tools that support xAPI, cmi5, or SCORM are crucial and allow authors or admins to directly upload content. Some authoring platforms have integrations with LMS and LXP, facilitating direct publication without any manual file transfers. Certain tools even come with inherent hosting capabilities. This is a significant advantage because the content lives in the cloud and publishing it becomes very simple. Moreover, a tool with hosting abilities benefits both content creation (the authors) and consumption (the learners), providing users with a range of publication options tailored to their requirements, including:

- the cloud
- social media
- any website
- the intranet.

Branding

Preserving your corporate identity and branding is another important aspect. While many authoring tools allow users to customize the design, including uploading specific backgrounds, setting fonts and selecting colours, such options can be challenging for SMEs. Some tools set a consistent branding template that, once approved, is applied to all educational content. This ensures SMEs, the course authors, can't make alterations. In our experience, this is the only way your branding will be applied correctly and consistently.

KEEPING THE VISION AND PRODUCT ALIGNED

One of our major challenges is ensuring that our vision and product are aligned. And that is not an easy task. A big challenge is determining what to build and what not to build.

A UI designer once told me (Kasper) that an average Microsoft Word user uses less than 3 per cent of the available functionality. With that in mind, we set out on our mission to uncover that crucial 3 per cent for a simple learning authoring, also known as a creator tool.

From this vantage point and keeping ease of use in mind, *less is more*. We didn't want to burden our tool with excessive features. Because no matter how intuitive or well designed they might be, each additional feature brings complexity. Every new addition risks making the tool less straightforward and intuitive. More importantly, any feature not in sync with our overarching vision and goals is a distraction.

We experienced firsthand that the moment people start to use your tool, you get a non-stop stream of suggestions for additions, improvements and changes. Yet, many of these often didn't align with our vision or objectives. But it's challenging to turn down a potential client who promises to become a customer upon the addition of feature A or B. Meanwhile, customer feedback is invaluable. And there's always the push and pull from customer-facing departments, often leaning toward features that cater to short-term gains rather than aligning with our long-term strategic goals. Navigating these challenges is a normal part of any product organization, but mastering it is truly challenging.

When we started designing Easygenerator, we knew it would disrupt the authoring market. We also planned two features that we believed would make an impact on the LMS market: course hosting and result tracking.

With course hosting, sharing your course with learners became as easy as sharing a YouTube video. We would handle the hosting and all the technical challenges that came with it. Authors could share their courses with a single click, through either a link or an embed code. In our view, this feature was critical for making EGL a success. But running a course outside of an LMS meant you wouldn't get any data on the learner's results.

That was why we added result tracking. We were planning to implement xAPI anyway because we wanted to use it for reporting and data insights purposes, among other things. Adding result tracking based on xAPI seemed like a natural extension.

By integrating course hosting and result tracking, we essentially incorporated two of the primary features of an LMS into our creator platform. We decided to offer these LMS features for free (also intending to make a bit of an impact on the LMS market), but we never intended to build a full-blown LMS. These features ended up attracting many customers who either didn't have an LMS or couldn't use their corporate LMS for certain groups of learners. With our tool they found not only a convenient way to create learning content but also got these added LMS features for sharing and measuring results. The plan was that when these customers wanted more features, like managing learners or course results, they'd buy an LMS and run Easygenerator courses from there. However, many began to ask these functionalities from us as they didn't want to purchase an LMS. Slowly, these requests began to form a (very basic and incomplete) LMS.

From a strategic and visionary standpoint, this was not a good direction. It diverted resources and focus and it wasn't enough for our customers, who kept asking for more. Looking back, we probably should have stuck with just the hosting and result-tracking features and not ventured into the LMS realm.

This lesson is relevant not only for product development but for any change management project, including your potential EGL project. It's crucial to have clear goals and stay consistent. If you get a request that doesn't align with your vision, saying 'no' is a sign of strength. For instance, if you're rolling out a democratized approach for EGL and suddenly get a request to also accommodate a regulated approach, our advice is to decline. It will lead you astray and cause you to lose focus. You can run both a democratized and a regulated approach simultaneously, but they should be managed separately, by different teams, not as a merged project.

Notes

1 Perring, D (2019) LXP: Why buyers might need to look closely into the next 'big thing' in learning tech?, LinkedIn. https://www.linkedin.com/pulse/lxp-why-buyers-might-need-look-closely-next-big-david-perring-flpi/ (archived at https://perma.cc/J76P-XTNE)

2 SCORM.com (nd) SCORM versions explained. Advanced Distributed Learning (ADL) initiative. https://scorm.com/scorm-explained/business-of-scorm/scorm-versions/?utm_source=google&utm_medium=natural_search (archived at https://perma.cc/CV32-7KRQ)

3 xAPI.com (nd) Project Tin Can requirements: What problems does it solve? Available at: https://xapi.com/project-tin-can-requirements/?utm_source=google&utm_medium=natural_search (archived at https://perma.cc/J5SV-VJA5) [Accessed 28 August 2023].

9

A framework for implementing Employee-generated Learning

We have developed an Employee-generated Learning framework that we also employ to assist our customers. This framework was formulated in collaboration with our customer contacts, L&D managers, thought leaders and advisory board members. The framework guides you through three evolution phases: the pilot, roll-out and operation.

The three phases for implementing EGL

The pilot phase

This is where you start your EGL journey. An EGL implementation is never a 'big bang roll-out' from the start. You need to discover what works and what doesn't in your organization. A successful pilot lays the groundwork for rolling out on a larger scale. By the end of the pilot, you can decide whether you want to continue with EGL in your organization. Moreover, you'll have clarity on what you aim to achieve with EGL and how best to reach those goals.

Organizations implementing the EGL pilot phase focus on testing and assessing the idea of EGL. A pilot allows you to learn about its effectiveness and its cultural fit. You can align your EGL approach with the business objectives and engage stakeholders. Furthermore, you'll develop the initial technical infrastructure and processes for content production and publication.

This stage emphasizes the importance of setting clear goals, developing a proof of concept, obtaining stakeholder buy-in, working with specific teams for trial, organizing the necessary tools and infrastructure, focusing on basic content creation and evaluating the pilot's success to determine the next steps for roll-out.

The roll-out phase

In this phase you extend the EGL approach from your pilot to a larger scale, applying the lessons learned during the pilot and expanding to other teams, projects and regions.

After a successful pilot phase, it's time to scale the idea. This involves spreading the word and expanding the reach of EGL within your organization. You'll need to identify new course authors, incorporate community support and adjust the technology you're using to support more authors, wider collaboration and a community infrastructure.

The objective is to dissolve silos, promoting a synergistic collaboration. You'll implement a structured approach to content creation and governance, introducing review cycles to continuously optimize the process. The ultimate goal is ensuring a smooth and effective expansion of EGL, reaching a broader audience and maximizing its organizational impact.

The operational phase

In this phase, you'll concentrate on the activities that will ensure a smooth EGL process in your organization, further embedding it into the system.

During the operational stage, your primary focus is on continuously maintaining and managing all aspects of EGL. This involves aligning and readjusting the strategy to stay in sync with business objectives, re-engaging stakeholders through effective communication and maintaining a stable and optimal infrastructure. Additionally, you'll consistently produce and evaluate content, apply community management practices for collaboration and set up user management

FIGURE 9.1 The three phases of EGL

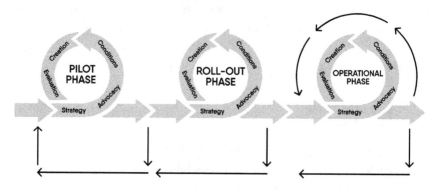

processes. Initiatives encouraging knowledge sharing become a formal part of everyone's duties. Strategic evaluations, using both tangible and intangible metrics, are conducted to calculate the ROI and gauge EGL's organizational impact.

Activities and attention points for each phase are categorized under five pillars or enablers: Strategy, Advocacy, Conditions, Creation and Evaluation – see Figure 9.1.

The components of EGL

Strategy

The Why. In this component, you delve into the reason and vision underlying EGL. When executed effectively, the strategy transforms from mere actions to a purpose-driven approach, offering direction, motivation and profound meaning. This strategy has the potential to influence and even reshape your organization's culture. It's vital to ensure that the EGL culture you cultivate aligns with and supports the organization's broader goals. Activities within the strategy component guide you in determining the best approach: a democratized or regulated EGL approach, or perhaps a mix of both. While the democratized approach emphasizes empowering and facilitating your SMEs, the regulated approach introduces greater control and top-down planning. A crucial outcome of this component involves setting clear objectives for each phase of implementation, while defining overarching EGL goals that align with the business objectives.

Advocacy

The Who. Focusing on the people integral to your process, this component emphasizes engagement and collaboration. Advocacy covers securing and managing stakeholder buy-in. To successfully implement EGL, you must collaborate with stakeholders outside of L&D and HR because for many stakeholders, learning, knowledge sharing and performance support might not be core activities. It's essential to promote, defend and support the ideas behind EGL, aiming to inspire and excite approvers, conduits, authors and other important stakeholders—ideally transforming them into EGL advocates.

Conditions

The How. This component ensures all foundational conditions for EGL are established. While tools and technologies play a role, alignment on processes and responsibilities is equally vital. For example, governance may or may not be an immediate requirement depending on the type of EGL implemented. Nonetheless, having the related setup helps to establish a plan if needed later. *The Why* and *The Who* are well defined, with outcomes seamlessly integrated into daily operations and organizational structures. Through the activities in this component, you're preparing the organization and infrastructure so you can achieve your goals. Your choices in tools and standards largely shape the infrastructure, creating a learning technology ecosystem applicable not just to EGL but to all learning initiatives.

Creation

The What. Here lies the heart of knowledge and experience creation and sharing. In this component, we describe what the content creation process can look like for each phase. For SMEs creating the learning and performance content, guidance and support come from the L&D team. It covers all that's needed to ensure optimal organization, aiming for content creation that leaves a positive imprint on the organization's overall performance.

Evaluation

The When. Evaluations must take place at the end of each iteration and phase (see Table 9.1). These evaluations serve to identify challenges and areas for improvement and inform the subsequent steps. This will help decide whether it's time to roll out this methodology into other areas or whether more iterations or an extended pilot are needed.

TABLE 9.1 Activities for each phase and component of EGL

	Pilot Phase	Roll-Out Phase	Operational Phase
Strategy	Set the goal and scope for the pilot.	Set the goals and milestones for the roll-out phase.	Set the long-term goals for EGL.
Advocacy	Get buy-in from pilot stakeholders and participants.	Get buy-in from stakeholders and participants.	Continue communication with stakeholders and keep them involved.
Conditions	Organize the tooling, processes, and infrastructure for the pilot.	Organize the tooling, processes, and infrastructure.	Make sure the conditions are stable and well maintained.
Creation	SMEs involved in the pilot begin content creation and sharing.	SME content creation and sharing spreads to the wider organization.	Content creation and sharing continues (often in a mixed regulated and democratized approach).
Evaluation	Evaluate the pilot results and decide on the next steps.	Evaluate after each phase or iteration and decide on the next steps.	Conduct periodical evaluations that will shape the next steps.

To conclude, the five components remain constant across the three phases. In every phase it's crucial to align EGL aims with business objectives and culture (strategy), to involve stakeholders through clear communication (advocacy), to ensure the right technology, processes and infrastructure are in place (conditions), to produce compelling and relevant content (creation) and to assess and refine the approach for defining the next step (evaluation).

In this chapter we identified the five fundamental components central to the EGL maturity model. Next, our attention shifted to the pilot, roll-out and operational phases to delve into the role these components fulfil. Recognizing that company size plays a pivotal role in EGL implementation, we outlined the strategies for large enterprises from those for small and medium enterprises. For adopting EGL in a large enterprise, keep reading. For adopting EGL in a small or medium enterprise, skip ahead to Chapter 11.

10

Employee-generated Learning for large enterprises

In large organizations with abundant resources and a global presence, implementing the EGL initiative often requires a more formal approach. Such organizations have complex structures, multiple departments and well-established learning and development functions.

The primary factors that influence EGL implementation in these large firms include:

1 **Organizational size and complexity**: Given the vastness of these firms with multiple entities, the primary goal should be to develop standardized frameworks and procedures. These can then be tailored to various departments or regions.

2 **Budget and resource availability**: Having adequate resources, which encompass a budget, dedicated staff and sophisticated technology, is vital for the successful scaling of EGL. The good news is that these are already in place. Now it's up to the L&D to champion and present the right business case for EGL.

EGL has the potential to change your organization. If you want to foster a culture of knowledge sharing, you need to make changes within the organization. Interestingly, for some businesses that incorporated EGL, this transformation was the overarching objective; they leveraged EGL only as a vehicle to drive this change.

Between 1997 and 2000, British Petroleum became one of the first companies to restructure to make knowledge sharing possible.[1] A case study illustrates how they promoted teamwork and open communication among the staff.[2] As a result of this change, they decided to change the company's organizational structure. Specifically, the organization changed into a federal setup with two main parts: a central core team for strategic decisions and separate business unit teams to work on their own, while following the rules set by the central core. This change fostered trust among employees and empowered them to control their knowledge-sharing activities.

CASE STUDY

Addressing different training needs at the right speed

A multinational French food-products company recognized that all their employees had unique learning needs. The most effective way they saw to meet these individual needs was by fostering a culture where employees could draw on each other's expertise and take charge of their own learning.

They successfully used EGL as the foundation for establishing this culture. SMEs now create a significant portion of the learning content without the direct involvement of the L&D department. This approach allows employees to capture and share their expertise swiftly, eliminating the need for numerous interviews or feedback sessions with L&D or third parties. And because employees have ownership of the content, they can update it just as quickly. This method has sparked a genuine interest in knowledge sharing and learning, laying the groundwork for a robust culture of both.

Two years post-EGL implementation, the company has over 500 content creators spanning more than 30 countries. One of the most substantial outcomes has been the cultivation of a knowledge-sharing culture. Today, local teams can produce and manage their content autonomously. The most significant advantage? Employees can tap into each other's expertise, no matter their location, ensuring they benefit from collective wisdom. In this system, the roles of the L&D and HR teams have evolved. Instead of merely producing content, they now play a pivotal role in nurturing and promoting the learning culture.

The pilot phase

Strategy

Find a high-profile team within your company to conduct the pilot with. Pick a team that has already had learning success and is trustworthy and capable in management's eyes. The pilot shouldn't be too elaborate or a long-running project. Start by determining the following:

- L&D challenge: the problem you're trying to solve and its context.
- Objectives: what you want to achieve with the pilot.
- Key players: the stakeholders — approvers, conduits and authors.
- EGL-related challenges: the list of possible challenges for EGL implementation.
- Plan: a strategy for engaging each group of stakeholders.
- Success indicators: measurable indicators of success for the pilot.

A SAMPLE EGL PROJECT

L&D challenge:

The centralized L&D team, primarily fluent in the head office's language, struggles to cater to the diverse linguistic demands of various branches. This has led to significant external spending. Regional SMEs, unwilling to wait, turn to third-party vendors in their respective countries.

Objectives:

- Grant SMEs and project owners more autonomy over regional learning content associated with knowledge sharing and performance support.
- Minimize dependency on external translation vendors.
- Reduce the spending with external vendors.
- Show that the external spend on content creation can be reduced.
- Show that SMEs are enabled to create training in their own time.

Key players:

- Approvers: business leaders.
- Conduits: department heads, team leaders.
- Authors: employees (SMEs).

EGL-related challenges:

- Challenges related to translation, publication and distribution.
- Transitioning from a PowerPoint mindset to an e-learning perspective.
- Conveying the idea that courses do not need to be perfect.
- Managing licence allocation issues (such as how many emails and passwords are required).
- Securing SMEs' buy-in.

Plan:

- Schedule a session with conduits in the learning teams to secure their buy-in.
- Schedule an SME launch session.
- All regional SME teams should have access to authoring tools and build learning content in their choice of language. These tools should also have localization capabilities.
- Plan for a quarterly business review with business leaders.
- The central L&D team can focus on managing strategy and processes.

Success indicators:

- The training team should invest no time in SME content creation.
- Achieve a 25 per cent reduction in spending, using one unit as a benchmark.
- Publish 30 courses.
- Attain an NPS score of 40+.
- Ensure content is released to at least five regions.

Advocacy

Connecting people is as important as collecting or creating content. The question is, who do you connect with and what is your message?

The first step is to map out the people involved in all three groups: approvers, conduits and authors. Once you know with whom you have to communicate, you need to create a clear elevator pitch and messaging for each group. EGL facilitators must work with all these groups and ensure that they're aligned and communicating.

Defining the right messaging is important as this will help mobilize change towards this new learning approach. To define your messaging, we recommend following the Head-Heart-Habit model, which will take you through three simple steps:

1 **Head:** What will appeal to people's logic about why this change is needed?

2 **Heart:** What will appeal to people's emotions about why this change is important for the future?

3 **Habit:** What will appeal to people's knowledge of what they need to do to support this change?

ENGAGING THE APPROVERS

Approvers, the C-level employees, are primarily interested in the expected and achieved business impact. It's important to keep them informed and engaged throughout the process. To define your messaging with approvers:

- HIGHLIGHT the alignment of EGL with the overall strategy and the value of data-driven insights in decision making (appealing to the 'head').

- EMPHASIZE that the L&D team's focus on priorities will be maintained, demonstrating efficient resource allocation and commitment to organizational goals (appealing to the 'heart').

- CLEARLY define responsibilities and scope among the L&D team and other stakeholders (appealing to 'habit').

Some key strategies:

- Have a kick-off meeting with the approvers to co-create the success plan. Ensure that all approvers sign off on the plan to establish commitment and alignment.
- Involve the approvers in the mid-way pilot review to provide visibility on the progress and allow them to share any concerns or areas of focus.
- Involve all approvers in the final pilot evaluation.

ENGAGING THE CONDUITS

Conduits, such as team leaders and department heads, are interested in understanding the benefits of EGL for themselves, their teams and the future. In your interactions with conduits, reflect on the existing challenges they face, how EGL can alleviate these, potential push-back from end users and strategies to mitigate this resistance. Bear in mind that your SMEs have responsibilities beyond content creation and conduits oversee them. If conduits remain unconvinced of EGL's merits, they might obstruct the process, perhaps by restricting content-creating time for authors. To define your messaging with conduits:

- emphasize the support for EGL as it aligns with the firm's overarching strategy, highlighting its benefits without incurring additional costs (appealing to the 'head')
- portray EGL as a necessary solution for effective learning and development (appealing to the 'heart')
- clearly communicate what needs to be shared and provide appropriate support channels for it (appealing to 'habit').

Some key strategies:

- Organize webinars to gain their buy-in and demonstrate how they can contribute to identifying end users.
- Arrange one-on-one meetings with the top three to five most important conduits, such as business leaders of large units, to create ambassadors for the EGL initiative.
- Keep conduits informed about the progress of the implementation.

ENGAGING THE AUTHORS

When engaging authors, the SMEs, it's important to provide them with the necessary resources, supporting their active participation. To define your messaging with authors:

- Highlight the benefits of ownership, freedom in content creation and quick implementation (appealing to the 'head').

- Emphasize the opportunity for authors to share their expertise and feel appreciated for their contributions, creating a sense of value and fulfilment (appealing to the 'heart').

- Provide internal recognition and support from the L&D team (appealing to 'habit').

Some key strategies:

- Create a centralized landing page about EGL on your intranet or communication platform. This landing page should serve as a comprehensive resource, including:

  o your message for the authors, highlighting the value and benefits of EGL

  o a brief functional description of the tools and processes involved in EGL

  o a link to self-paced onboarding materials to help authors get started.

- Send a launch email to the identified potential authors (identified by L&D), introducing them to EGL and inviting them to join the initial user group.

- Announce EGL in your organization's newsletter and recurring meetings to create awareness and encourage participation.

LAUNCH EMAIL

Dear SME,

Share your expertise effortlessly with EGL, the innovative solution for knowledge sharing. We've provided EGL tools to all employees at no additional cost. Choose EGL for you and your team to address recurring questions or common errors. Capture them once and for all!

- No more repetitive questions or one-off sessions. Create engaging e-learning courses and resources to reach a larger audience.

- Not an e-learning expert? No problem. Our user-friendly tools and ready-to-use templates make it quick and simple for you to share your knowledge.

- Keep your content up to date with ease.

Join us in revolutionizing knowledge sharing across our organization.

Conditions

Your implementation of EGL will vary based on the approach you want to adopt. In large organizations, a regulated approach means setting up guidelines, policies and governance processes to ensure quality, consistency and compliance in EGL initiatives. If you opt for a democratized approach, you'll still require guidelines and policies. However, the governance process might be simpler or, in some instances, non-existent.

You want a tool that allows you to start quickly with your pilot. SaaS is ideal in this case because you can kick off in mere hours or days, unlike installing software on company servers which could take weeks or months. That's why a SaaS tool is often the preferred choice for a pilot. Post-pilot, you can stick with SaaS or transition to an installed solution. Plus, with SaaS, the IT department's involvement is minimal since vendors mostly handle it. But ensure the tool aligns with your organization's security and privacy guidelines, which will require IT approval.

Regulated EGL approaches typically involve a review process to ensure the didactical quality and accuracy of the content. These are two very different reviews! If needed, it will be someone from L&D that will check the didactical quality. The accuracy of the content needs to be checked by other SMEs. Select a tool that has both options.

Given the multitude of tools available to employees in sizable organizations – such as LMS, LXP, Slack, Teams, Zoom, Wiki pages, team pages, shared drives, SharePoint – SMEs will expect to share their content through some or all of these channels. Therefore, when selecting tools for knowledge sharing, ensure they are compatible with the various platforms used within the organization.

Creation

Here, you can focus on empowering creators to share their expertise and knowledge for the pilot. It's essential to recognize that they are not learning specialists. We always advise starting with a kick-off and onboarding session with the SMEs involved in the pilot. Our standard programme includes:

1 Group introductions.
2 Making sure everybody has access to the tooling.
3 The importance of defining your audience and learning objectives.
4 Guidelines for creating content.
5 Tool demos.
6 The governance process, quality checks and publication process.
7 Q&A session.

We've created a supportive tool for SMEs that helps them create a course outline, the Outline Builder. It guides the authors in taking an actionable approach to identifying the content that ties in directly with their job. It does so through three steps:

1 Authors define the purpose, setting the context of the course. (This becomes the learning objective).

2 Based on the objective, authors then identify the key takeaways. (These become the topics or sections of the course.)

3 Authors structure these topics by mapping the content type including how-tos, open-pages, procedures and so on. (These become the content pages within the sections.)

After the third step, our tool transforms all this information into a course outline.

Instructional designers might assist in content creation, but their role depends on your choices. Their involvement can range from helping set objectives to coaching SMEs in content creation, but they should not take over the responsibility for creating content.

Develop a clear and concise definition or decision tree to determine which e-learnings require L&D approval (e.g. ISO, compliance, health and safety courses) and which should be created by SMEs. Ensure that the L&D team and SMEs are familiar with these criteria.

Create a checklist to encourage authors to adhere to quality guidelines and make this easily accessible. The checklist can include items such as:

- defined learning objectives
- brand guideline adherence
- peer reviews
- didactical approval
- content lifespan considerations.

For publishing, establish clear protocols. Decide whether SMEs can self-publish and if not, appoint admins to facilitate this.

Evaluation

Use your company's analytics or LMS to track how many employees have benefited from EGL courses. Also, include a satisfaction survey within each course to get feedback on how much employees liked the courses. Here's a list of metrics that will convey your pilot usage of EGL:

- Number of authors/creators.
- Number of editors/reviewers.
- Number of content pieces created.
- Frequency of creation and sharing.
- Frequency of drop-offs.
- Frequency of log-ins.
- Data on content usage.

Launching EGL can inspire SMEs in your organization to create their own training. Take note of any additional employee-generated e-learning initiatives during the pilot phase. These initiatives can be valuable for future development and implementation. If you're following a democratized approach, encourage your authors to create content after the pilot. If you choose a more regulated approach, create a platform or forum where employees can submit their e-learning ideas. Review the submissions and identify promising initiatives to develop further and implement.

Engage in surveys and conversations with the SMEs participating in the pilot phase. Ask them about their experience creating EGL. For instance, how much time did it save them? This will help highlight the effectiveness of EGL. As another example, have interviews or group discussions with course authors to gather feedback on their experience. Ask about the challenges they faced, the benefits they gained and any suggestions they have for improvement. Additionally, distribute a survey to gather feedback on the relevance, clarity and overall quality of the EGL content. Consider a few strategic questions that will help you decide on the next steps.

POST-PILOT SURVEY QUESTIONS FOR THE EGL IMPLEMENTATION TEAM

- Does EGL add value to the organization and support its strategic goals? (*Value Addition*)

- What are the missing components required for a successful EGL rollout? (*Components Evaluation*)

- How do we evaluate the progress of EGL implementation and readiness for the operations stage? (*Progress Tracking*)

- To what extent have employees adopted EGL and who are the successful contributors among them? (*Employee Adoption*)

Based on the survey data, you can then decide whether you should continue with EGL or not. And if you do, what are your goals and your plans?

The roll-out phase

Strategy

Large firms have the advantage of conducting comprehensive pilot programmes involving diverse teams and locations. They analyze data from the pilot to identify best practices, successful approaches and potential challenges. This analysis enables them to refine the roll-out plan based on broader insights.

Engaging business leaders from different departments or business units is crucial. The rollout strategy involves presenting data-driven results from the pilot to gain support from top executives. You need these leaders to actively advocate EGL across the organization, emphasizing alignment with the company's overall strategic goals. Additionally, you need further funding and support, so develop a comprehensive sponsorship plan with involvement from various stakeholders, including executives, managers and key influencers.

Breaking organizational silos in large firms is often a complex task. However, they leverage dedicated cross-functional teams, regular communication channels and technology platforms to foster collaboration. These platforms encourage knowledge sharing, discussion forums and collaborative projects, enhancing EGL's impact.

Stakeholder characteristics and activities

As the emphasis is clearly on getting buy-in from stakeholders for additional funding or support, you can use the standard four types of stakeholders as a starting point.[3] This will help you devise your sponsorship plan for the EGL roll-out.

LOW INTEREST AND LOW INFLUENCE STAKEHOLDERS

These stakeholders have low enthusiasm in the project and possess limited power to influence its success.

Activities:

- Limited communication needed.
- Conduct surveys to gather input from this group.
- Share high-level plan updates on the website.

LOW INTEREST AND HIGH INFLUENCE STAKEHOLDERS

These stakeholders have minimal interest in the project but possess significant power to influence its success; however, they still play an active role in impacting the project.

Activities:

- Keep them informed of critical information.
- Respond to specific requests or concerns.

HIGH INTEREST AND LOW INFLUENCE STAKEHOLDERS

These stakeholders have a strong interest in the project but lack the power to significantly impact its success.

Activities:

- Conduct one-on-one interviews or small group sessions to understand their perspectives and needs.
- Share detailed plan information.

HIGH INTEREST AND HIGH INFLUENCE STAKEHOLDERS

These stakeholders have a strong interest in the project and possess significant power to influence its success. Therefore, they are very influential.

Activities:

- Include them in strategy sessions for planning.
- Develop a comprehensive communication plan.
- Share in-depth project plan details.
- Engage in ongoing two-way communication.
- Prioritize their needs and interests.
- Consider their opinions and recommendations.

GENERAL ACTIVITIES

- Share the plan with all stakeholders.
- Hold town hall sessions for key stakeholders.
- Update the website with the organization's vision, mission and values for low-interest stakeholders.

- Adapt communication based on feedback and needs.
- Ensure plan actions are completed.
- Engage the leadership team in plan implementation.

You might ask, how do you know who is in which category? It's true that influence is a subjective topic and our evaluation of a certain stakeholder might be different from yours. This is crucial to identify and assess the interest and influence levels of stakeholders. Classify your stakeholders based on their role or position and gain insight into their priorities and goals. This will help you greatly in tailoring your engagement strategy.

Advocacy

Knowledge-sharing efforts in large industries often don't receive the necessary investment in marketing and promotion. This is essential for scaling.[4] Effective marketing can increase awareness and enthusiasm for EGL, allowing for broader team implementation. Much like with EGL, it's crucial to enhance messaging and recognition programmes to maintain motivation.

Engage executives and senior leaders in promoting EGL, underscoring their role as EGL champions. The champions' role should be clearly defined. Seek out individuals genuinely enthusiastic about EGL and its potential benefits. Engage a diverse group of internal stakeholders – from department heads and managers to employees in various locations – to cultivate momentum and backing for EGL. Appoint EGL ambassadors or advocates across teams and departments to foster participation and zeal. Additionally, circulate monthly data reports to all decision makers. This ensures a transparent view of progress and lets them gauge the influence of the EGL initiative with ease.

Adopt a phased approach to EGL implementation, targeting different departments or business units with tailored EGL initiatives. Showcase successful EGL case studies in various departments to inspire others to join in.

Introduce a formal recognition system that values EGL input. While this can take the form of monetary or performance-driven rewards, it's important to ensure your SMEs are acknowledged by their peers for their expertise. Make sure their contributions are in the spotlight and attribute the content to them rightfully.

RECOGNITION ACTIVITIES

- Leadership endorsement
  - Eligibility: top EGL advocates
  - Details: senior leaders publicly endorse top EGL advocates during company events
  - Reward: public acknowledgement and visibility
- Virtual wall of fame
  - Eligibility: exceptional EGL contributors
  - Details: showcasing the profiles and contributions of top EGL contributors
  - Reward: feature on company intranet or website
- Spotlight features
  - Eligibility: successful EGL contributors
  - Details: featuring EGL success stories in newsletters and communications
  - Reward: public recognition and appreciation
- Leadership endorsement
  - Eligibility: highly active contributors
  - Details: selecting teams with highest contributors
  - Reward: monetary incentives or a token of appreciation
- Leadership endorsement
  - Eligibility: all contributors
  - Details: make sure the name and details of the author are visible for the learners, as this will give the SMEs recognition for their work as well as responsibility for the content
  - Reward: general recognition as an expert

Moreover, create a comprehensive messaging plan that emphasizes EGL's strategic importance and its role in aligning with the company's vision and business strategy. Use multiple communication channels, such as town hall meetings, webinars and company-wide emails, to reach a diverse audience.

MESSAGING PLAN

- Announcing the EGL roll-out
  - When: at the start of the roll-out phase
  - Channel: company-wide communication
  - Audience: all employees
  - Owner: HR/L&D department
- EGL endorsements from executives
  - Frequency: throughout the roll-out phase
  - Channel: company meetings or the intranet
  - Audience: managers, team leaders, employees
  - Owner: HR/L&D department and/or senior leaders
- Department-specific updates
  - Frequency: regularly during the roll-out phase
  - Channel: department meetings and/or emails
  - Audience: specific department or team members
  - Owner: HR/L&D department and/or department heads
- Company-specific updates
  - Frequency: ongoing throughout EGL
  - Channel: company newsletters and/or the intranet
  - Audience: all employees
  - Owner: HR/L&D department and/or EGL champions

Conditions

With the foundational tools and processes in place to nurture the EGL ecosystem, it's time to take it to the next level, beyond content creation and storage.

First, strengthen and grow internal processes. As more authors and creators join from various departments, it becomes crucial to put in place governance, user management and role planning and encourage collaboration. For measuring the success of the EGL initiative, use data analytics and performance indicators. These will monitor both content quality and the performance of the creators, pinpointing what's working well and what needs improvement. Instead of waiting for a project's end to evaluate, think about running an interim health check. This check, done midway through the project, addresses potential issues early on, collecting feedback from users and sponsors.[5]

Second, as EGL matures, consolidating various tools and platforms is key. Seamless integration with systems like LMSs, LXPs and collaborative tools (such as Microsoft Teams or Slack) is crucial. Given you'll be dealing with multiple vendors, establish solid IT policies and service agreements to ensure smooth operations, safety and support. Following a clear vendor selection process will help in making well-informed choices, paving the way for future EGL undertakings in your company.

Creation

In any sizable company, translating, localizing and creating courses for specific audiences present immediate opportunities. These are the easy targets to scale up your content development with SMEs.

The content creation in the pilot phase starts in the company's main language or, often, in English. If you allow people to create content in their native language, you'll find it easier to recruit SMEs; additionally, most people learn better in their native language. However, for the benefit of a wider audience, this content needs translation. Automated translations from certain authoring tools can help, but they require verification before release. You can use your SMEs for this task as well. This makes a great case for EGL because typically a lot of money is spent on translation services.

To make content even more relevant, go a step beyond just translation: localize it. This means adjusting content to fit local cultures, norms and regulations. The same SMEs who handle translation are ideally positioned to manage this.

L&D departments often find it expensive to create courses for specific, smaller audiences, leading to a poor return on investment. This is where SMEs become invaluable, often representing the areas where EGL thrives the most. Many L&D teams face a content creation backlog. Working with SMEs can alleviate this. An instructional designer collaborating with SMEs produces content more swiftly than working solo. EGL is an effective way to reduce that backlog. Moreover, content needn't always be in the form of extensive courses. microlearning, smaller, practical chunks of information, can often be more effective and easier for SMEs to create. Tools to support such content, like FAQs, best practices and how-tos, are becoming more common in many authoring tools. Encouraging SMEs to start with this kind of content is a good step, with more comprehensive courses coming later if necessary.

More ideas on where you can scale up further:

- Support and empower creators by providing additional (snappy) resources and training.
- Use successful pilot projects as templates for future content creation.
- Make EGL an integral part of the standard learning roadmap for all employees.

KNOWLEDGE TAXONOMIES

Should SMEs need inspiration, guide them towards content ideas from knowledge taxonomies.[6] The knowledge taxonomies categorize knowledge based on the nature of content:

- **Know-how**: practical procedural knowledge and skills gained through experience. For example, a medical coder performing transcript and code mapping on a complex database.
- **Know-who**: knowing the right people with specific expertise or knowledge. For example, a project manager connecting the right team members to address project challenges effectively.

- **Know-what**: factual knowledge about something. For example, a data scientist who has a deep understanding of data methods and patterns.

- **Know-why**: understanding the reasons or principles behind a phenomenon or action. For example, an engineer who comprehends the scientific principles governing the operation of a complex machine.

- **Know-what-if**: the ability to anticipate and analyse potential scenarios and outcomes. For example, a financial analyst assessing the impact of different economic factors on investment decisions.

- **Know-where**: knowing the location of specific information, resources or places. For example, a customer success executive quickly finds information on competitors in a shared drive.

- **Know-when**: understanding the appropriate timing for certain actions or decisions. For example, a marketing manager planning promotional campaigns to coincide with peak sales seasons.

Furthermore, make sure that the SME is responsible not only for the creation but also for the maintenance of the content. They should feel they own the content; if you achieve that, the SME will automatically update the content if anything changes in the day-to-day practice.

A key tip is to establish a straightforward naming convention for e-learnings. This will allow for easy identification of topics and functional areas and will also help track effectiveness and popularity of courses.

Another idea is to create a community platform where authors can share knowledge, identify existing content and find inspiration for EGL examples. You can also designate a specific area within the LMS for courses created through EGL, ensuring a user-friendly experience and easy access.

Lastly, set up a recurring training plan for new and existing authors. This training plan ensures that authors receive the necessary support and guidance throughout the EGL process, enabling them to onboard, develop their skills and feel supported.

Evaluation

To ensure the effectiveness of your EGL initiative, base your evaluations on concrete data. Below are two metrics you should consider, among others.

CONTRIBUTIONS ANALYSIS

- Monitor the frequency and regularity of content contributions to the EGL idea.
- Assess the relevance and quality of content submissions from SMEs.
- Demonstrate engagement levels by showcasing active participation and knowledge sharing.

COMMUNITY ENGAGEMENT

- Track the number of times courses or resources are accessed.
- Measure the average time users spend on different content pages; this will give insights into which topics garner more interest.
- Monitor how often content is shared as this is a direct indication of its utility and pertinence.
- Record the number of different departments and global regions participating to understand the breadth of the initiative's impact.
- Track the engagement metrics for content in languages other than English to ensure inclusivity and diversity in participation.
- Monitor the number of likes and comments on content pages to get a grasp on user satisfaction levels and the depth of interaction.

By this mid-stage of EGL implementation, you can start monitoring early signs of impact through job-performance indicators such as improvement in employee skills and increased operational productivity. Apart from these tangible metrics, both creators and administrators should focus on some of the more nuanced aspects of the project. These include addressing any significant challenges faced during the initiative and creating an environment in which participants feel comfortable discussing and learning from their mistakes. These will be valuable lessons for future projects or phases.

The timeframe for the rollout phase can vary based on several factors, such as the company's culture or size. It's essential to check in and evaluate progress when milestones are achieved. A general recommendation is to conduct evaluations every 3–6 months.

It's also important to note that the roll-out phase might often overlap with the operation phase. For segments of the project where the roll-out has been completed, you can move on to the operation phase. Meanwhile, sections that are still in progress or have yet to begin will continue to be part of the roll-out phase.

The operational phase

Strategy

Most organizations will have proven the idea by this stage, got advocacy, raised awareness and scaled to other departments. It's time to integrate EGL into the overall business strategy and day-to-day operations. This means:

- Establishing a strong connection between the data insights of EGL initiatives and the achievement of business objectives.

- Allocating a budget, time and resources for EGL in business plans others.

- Fostering a cross-functional collaboration among business units to engage in knowledge sharing, leading to innovative practices, products, services and more.

- Implementing a formal knowledge-sharing policy across different teams and departments.

- Including EGL in the employees' quarterly plans; tying in their creation efforts with future promotions.

Overall, you need to develop a cohesive and coordinated central strategy for EGL implementation across the organization. If other initiatives are happening in the firm, align and connect as well. This way, the EGL initiative will be perceived as something that *complements* other initiatives rather than a standalone investment. Make the effort to identify areas where the operations could improve with EGL, determining specific areas for improvement.

Advocacy

As EGL evolves, it may disrupt the status quo, presenting new approaches to content and knowledge management. This evolution translates to a change management effort, which requires:

- continuous support and guidance from senior leaders
- constant communication between different stakeholders
- publicizing success stories to emphasize the power of EGL
- providing awareness training at all levels to remind employees of its benefits.

Advocacy for EGL is not just about convincing stakeholders of its importance. Rather, it's about consistently reinforcing and reminding them of its value. So, make sure you re-engage with the stakeholders on a regular basis. Don't take their support for granted but keep nurturing it. Align their interests with EGL's success and keep them informed about EGL's progress, demonstrating its impact on the organizational goals. This ongoing communication will ensure that EGL remains a priority and has the necessary support and funding for further growth.

Consider that stakeholders, like L&D heads, have multiple projects and initiatives. To ensure EGL's success, find ways to complement existing initiatives as we mentioned previously. For example, if blended learning is being implemented, EGL can contribute to the digital content part of the blended learning. Linking EGL with other initiatives will make it feel supported and integrated.

Conditions

You need to identify areas that need improvement. Ensure advanced interconnected IT systems that support content distribution, integrate with other systems and provide security infrastructure and analytics tied to business goals. Regularly evaluate your toolkit and decide whether it remains the best solution. If your systems lack certain features, challenge vendors; many will listen.

Form a centre of excellence with experts from different branches to manage content and data, monitor operations and extend EGL benefits to untouched areas. As mentioned in the operation phase's advocacy component, new roles like 'facilitators' are emerging. Explore this option.

Develop additional training on practical topics such as conducting pilots, addressing objections and overseeing the EGL ecosystem, enabling business units and team leaders to manage EGL without L&D's constant support.

Creation

During the pilot stage, guidance on content creation is crucial. For L&D, the focus will move towards managing the EGL process. Often, EGL becomes a blend of regulated and democratized methods. If there are gaps in the content portfolio, L&D should task SMEs with creating the courses to fill these gaps – more of a regulated approach. And much of the content creation will now be led by SMEs who by this point are more skilled in designing, writing and maintaining content – leaning towards a democratized approach.

Content from the regulated approach typically gets uploaded to the LMS, while content initiated by SMEs often goes to the LXP. Generally, SMEs can't publish on the LMS, but they can on the LXP. L&D's task is to supervise this process and mentor the SMEs, as well as guiding them through the content creation process. Here, we provide a checklist for SMEs to help with course creation.

COURSE CREATION CHECKLIST FOR SMES

1 Pre-creation:

   o Define your topic and audience.

   o Check for existing learning material on the topic.

2 Introduction:

- Define the course goal.
- Specify what learners need to do to pass the course.

3 Learning objectives:

- Create actionable and measurable learning objectives.

4 Questions:

- Create questions that cover all learning objectives.
- Provide meaningful feedback for the questions.

5 Course content:

- Only create content that will answer the questions.
- Remove any unnecessary content. (When in doubt, leave it out!)
- Verify the accuracy of facts and provide appropriate references.
- Ensure the course follows a logical order.
- Use examples that accurately reflect real-life contexts.
- Proofread the text for errors.
- Send out the course to fellow experts for review.

6 Media assets:

- Ensure the images accurately represent the course material.
- Use audio meaningfully; avoid narration of the on-screen text.
- Include relevant videos.
- Provide introductory text and follow-up questions for the videos.

At this stage, SMEs should independently produce, publish and update content, making L&D a facilitator rather than a roadblock.

Be aware that you can function in multiple phases simultaneously. If you're expanding EGL to new countries, departments or significant new user groups that might have been overlooked in prior phases, start these efforts as pilots. It's normal to have multiple initiatives running in parallel across various stages.

By now you've built an active community of practice. Support these groups by establishing online communities for mutual assistance and guidance.

Evaluation

At this point, EGL should be integrated into your organizational processes. However, some stakeholders may question its value and effectiveness. Analyzing both tangible and intangible benefits is key to evaluating the investment returns from EGL. Start by focusing on intangible benefits, such as improved employee morale, better customer service and fewer complaints. Eventually, you'll need to quantify the impact, which is where ROI comes into play. Calculating ROI is complex and involves a deep understanding of the costs related to EGL.

The initial step is to have a thorough overview of all EGL-associated costs, which includes L&D's efforts, investment in tools and time devoted by SMEs.

The easy part of calculating ROI is the savings you have made. The cost of content and translations that used to be done by third parties and now are created in-house is a good start.

An easier part of determining ROI is identifying the savings. The costs saved from creating content in-house, which used to be outsourced, provide a starting point. When third-party vendors are involved in content creation, this becomes evident. But it isn't possible to measure the effort for every course and determine the ROI for each. A sensible method is to examine a select set of courses across various topics and sizes, understand the effort invested in their creation and then contrast that with the effort if SMEs weren't involved. The objective is to deduce an average saving per course or per learning hour. Once you have this average, calculating the total savings becomes straightforward: multiply these savings with the actual number of courses or hours produced. This angle of ROI primarily zooms in on cost savings.

Value creation is much more challenging to calculate. It is almost impossible to link any learning initiative and productivity directly.

The closest way in which this can be achieved is with performance support content. If you can determine – for instance by interviewing learners – how much time these assets have saved on average, you can convert that to a cost. For formal courses, this is not possible. There are other complex ways to determine the ROI for courses, but these can be speculative at best. It's not uncommon to find that the savings, combined with the effects of performance support, already surpass the costs associated with EGL. In such scenarios, you can present the number of courses created and learning hours spent on them as a benefit that you do not quantify further. Some of our customers only report that they now can create X times more content, X times faster and with X per cent fewer L&D staff. While not offering an ROI, it is still a clear indication of the effectiveness of EGL.

Notes

1 IvyPanda (nd) British Petroleum Company's knowledge management case study. Available at: https://ivypanda.com/essays/british-petroleum-companys-knowledge-management/#:~:text=Overview%20of%20Bp (archived at https://perma.cc/K7LG-BXPS) (Accessed 11 September 2023).
2 Kurt, A, Gorelick, C and Milton, N (2004) *Performance Through Learning: Knowledge management in practice*, The Netherlands: Routledge.
3 Project Management Institute (2017) *A guide to the Project Management Body of Knowledge* (PMBOK guide) (6th ed), USA: Project Management Institute
4 Produção, G, Arantes, L, Martinelli, O, Viegas, T and Rohenkohl, J (2021) Maturity and level of knowledge management in the company: An application of Nonaka and Takeuchi model and Fuzzy Logic, *Gestão & Produção*, 28, 10.1590/1806-9649-2020v28e5305 (archived at https://perma.cc/4JQQ-C97C)
5 Kurt, A, Gorelick, C and Milton, N (2004) *Performance Through Learning: Knowledge management in practice*, The Netherlands: Routledge.
6 Kowalczyk, A and Nogalski, B (2007) *Management of Knowledge. Concept and tools*, Warsaw: Print DIFIN.

11

Employee-generated Learning for small and medium enterprises

The implementation of Employee-generated Learning in small and medium enterprises differs from that in large organizations. On one hand, there's often more agility and flexibility; on the other, resources might be a constraint.

A less formal approach to EGL is often suitable for small and medium-sized enterprises. Start small and then progressively expand its scope within the organization. Most small and medium enterprises favour a more democratized approach over a strictly regulated one. It's also common to find either a very small learning department or none at all, which provides its distinct challenges.

In Chapter 9, we identified the five core components of the EGL framework. We emphasized that organizations need the right technology, support from senior management, governance and privacy processes and so on. Small and medium-sized firms might not possess all of these prerequisites. In some cases, all they have may be an experimental mindset and the motivation to kick things off.

CASE STUDY
Low-budget, high-impact L&D initiatives

Balamurugan runs a small edtech startup in India. Despite limited resources and a tight budget for formal training, he crafted a cost-effective learning strategy to foster growth within his team. He knew that his team had a lot of valuable knowledge, so he encouraged them to share it. Top performers became mentors and creators; they guided colleagues and helped them upskill. This created a collaborative and supportive culture in the company.

He told his team, 'If a Google research takes more than 30 minutes, ask a colleague!' And he told us, 'Besides shadowing seniors in projects, we encourage newbies to observe the seniors to understand the company culture. When a senior records and shares lessons learned, it showcases and promotes our knowledge (and idea) sharing culture.'[1]

Balamurugan didn't stop there. He consulted external industry experts about overcoming the company's challenges. Beyond that, team members were encouraged to leverage books, online courses and research journals for self-learning. This allowed them to expand their knowledge at their own pace and keep training costs low.

As the company grew and secured more funding, Balamurugan introduced new processes and governance. He put in place basic regulations to protect sensitive information and ensure the company's integrity, while still prioritizing knowledge sharing and mentoring. These rules emphasized the need to keep high standards in learning, making sure the knowledge shared was reliable, accurate and useful for professional growth. As the company expanded, Balamurugan saw the importance of a framework to support the team's ongoing learning, making sure it matched the company's main goals. Through Balamurugan's approach to learning and development, his small firm thrived in an industry dominated by giants.

The pilot phase

Strategy

Similar to large organizations, small and medium firms must also begin their EGL initiative by defining a pilot with specific topics. With smaller companies we often see that the initiation of EGL stems from the need to solve a particular problem. A very common problem is when an organization has a very small learning department or none at all and it cannot fulfil the requests for learning material. The need to retain organizational knowledge is another popular reason that has smaller companies looking into EGL.

A SAMPLE EGL PROJECT

L&D challenge:

There is a need for learning and support material but no or a very small learning department.

Objectives:

- Optimize using limited resources for training and development initiatives.
- Empower the organization's SMEs to create and share learning content.
- Establish a decentralized approach to learning and development.
- Start with one or two teams and one or two concrete organizational needs.

Key players:

- Approvers: founders, partners, management team and team leads.
- Enablers: SMEs.

EGL-related challenges:

- Limited L&D and training budgets.
- Lack of dedicated L&D resources.
- Limited time availability from SMEs; content creation is low on their priority list.

Plan:

- Seek support from leadership to allocate necessary resources for the pilot phase.
- Collaborate with managers and team leaders to identify specific training needs.
- Engage SMEs from various departments to contribute to creating learning content.
- Identify SMEs within the organization who can contribute to the pilot phase.
- Provide quick training and support to SMEs using creation/authoring tools.

- Establish a platform or system for content creation and sharing.
- Conduct regular meetings or workshops to ensure collaboration and knowledge sharing among SMEs.
- Set up a feedback mechanism to gather insights and improvement suggestions from pilot participants.
- Set up recognition programmes to motivate employees.

Success indicators:

- SMEs create and publish a minimum of 10 courses.
- EGL is implemented in at least two key departments or teams.

Advocacy

Connecting people is as important as collecting or creating content. The question is, who do you connect with and what is your message?

The first step is to map out the people involved into two groups: approvers and enablers. Once you know with whom you have to communicate, you need to create a clear elevator pitch and messaging for each group. EGL facilitators must work with all these groups and ensure that they're aligned and communicating.

Defining the right messaging is important, as this will help mobilize change towards this new learning approach. To define your messaging, we recommend following the Head-Heart-Habit model, which will take you through three simple steps:

1 **Head:** What will appeal to people's logic about why this change is needed?

2 **Heart:** What will appeal to people's emotions about why this change is important for the future?

3 **Habit:** What will appeal to people's knowledge of what they need to do to support this change?

The advantage with smaller organizations is that there are fewer stakeholders to manage.

ENGAGING THE APPROVERS

The approvers are the founders, partners, management team and team leads. To define your messaging with them:

- Highlight how EGL's cost-effective strategy aligns with small firms' objectives, maximizing limited resources and promoting employee development within budget.

- Position EGL as a strategic investment that cultivates a rapid learning culture in line with business evolution.

- Clearly outline the areas where EGL can have the most impact, such as specific projects and teams.

Some key strategies:

- Organize a targeted kick-off meeting with all approvers to outline the success roadmap. Aim for interactive discussions and ensure alignment.

- If possible, involve the management team in creating courses.

- Maintaining a more direct and personal approach to engaging stakeholders is key.

- Hold a direct line of communication and promptly address any concerns or areas of focus.

- Conduct regular progress updates through brief meetings or emails to keep approvers informed about the progress of the EGL implementation.

ENGAGING THE ENABLERS

The enablers are the authors, or in other words, the SMEs. To define your messaging with them:

- Emphasize the value of author contributions, how these will empower other employees and how their knowledge will be valued and utilized within the organization.

- Provide authors with resources and support for creating and delivering content.

Some key strategies:

- Develop a short and informative EGL overview document, highlighting the value and benefits of EGL for authors. Share this document via email or a shared drive, ensuring easy access for all authors.
- Use a targeted approach. Reach out to specific teams or departments directly involved in the EGL initiative and invite them to join the initial user group.
- Instead of a centralized landing page, create a dedicated email address or communication channel in Teams, Yammer or Slack where authors can directly reach out with questions and receive support.
- Establish a small and close-knit community of authors through regular in-person or virtual meetings, where they can share success stories, ask questions and support each other.

Conditions

- Identify key individuals responsible for EGL initiatives, such as the HR coordinator or a designated EGL champion.
- Appoint SMEs in different departments for creating and reviewing e-learning.
- Ensure effective communication channels are in place.
- Secure the necessary tools. If there's no existing learning software, look for authoring tools that have some learner facilities for hosting courses and results tracking. This will allow for a smoother start.

Creation

Employees often go the extra mile to support EGL and create content, in addition to their daily responsibilities. Acknowledge this and provide the necessary guidance and resources to help SMEs get the most out of the time they spend on the EGL initiative.

Here's what to do in the creation stage:

- Provide user-friendly and straightforward templates, guidelines and tools.
- Provide information on accessing internal documents, project files, solutions, diagrams, videos and more.
- Don't focus on perfection and stray away from complexity. Guide SMEs' content scope with questions like:
  - What knowledge or skills are needed to perform this task?
  - What are the primary obstacles in executing this task?
  - What foundational knowledge, processes or technical skills are required?
  - Who else is knowledgeable in this area?
  - How will this content benefit the learners?
- Share short yet powerful resources like:
  - checklists for everyday best practices
  - lessons from past mistakes
  - how-tos that explain processes or procedures.
- Introduce other experts within their teams.
- Share success stories through videos or stories.
- To stimulate creativity, provide sample content as inspiration.
- Decide whether certain topics or courses need governance; set these up if required.
- Ensure that the authors take ownership of the material they produce, updating and maintaining this as needed.

Evaluation

Often, small and medium firms evaluate success using informal indicators, such as the applicability of content and engagement levels.

Collect feedback from supervisors or team leaders to assess the applicability of EGL content for employees' specific roles in day-to-day tasks.

Encourage employees to share real-life examples that showcase how employee-generated content helped them. Spotlight moments where EGL insights played a key role in problem solving or decision making.

After the pilot's conclusion, a decision will be needed on whether to fully adopt EGL. Many smaller organizations that opt to continue often lean towards a more democratized approach.

Due to flat organizational structures and quick decision making, most small and medium-sized firms complete the pilot phase relatively quickly.

The roll-out phase

Strategy

In many instances, EGL initiatives grow organically (to some extent). However, it's essential to publicize them to ensure awareness. Additionally, the management team should actively support and convey its message. A more structured approach is also an option: you might roll out the EGL initiative department-wise, hold kick-off sessions for each department and discuss potential topics for learning material with the SMEs.

You may have conducted the pilot on a smaller scale, involving a limited number of employees or just one department. Regardless of its size, closely analyze the pilot's results, extracting valuable insights for the broader roll-out. Adjust your strategy based on these insights.

Advocacy

Advocacy can be more personal and intimate than in large corporations. Engage directly with business owners, department heads and employees to rally support for EGL. Highlight early successes from the pilot phase to boost enthusiasm and participation. Encourage employees to become EGL champions, emphasizing its advantages to colleagues and within teams. Additionally, crafting a coherent messaging plan is crucial. A sample of such a plan can be seen in Table 11.1.

It is also important to establish a recognition plan. Cultivate a culture of appreciation and praise, where employee contributions are celebrated within the close team environment. This will lead to a sense of camaraderie and mutual support in EGL endeavours. See a sample recognition plan in Table 11.2.

TABLE 11.1 Sample messaging plan

Message	Frequency	Channel	Audience	Owner
EGL kick-off announcement	At the start of EGL	Team meetings/ emails	All employees	HR department
Personalized appreciation	Ongoing throughout EGL	Direct communication	Individual contributors	Team managers
Sharing EGL impact	Regularly during EGL	Informal gatherings	All employees	Team managers
Employee spotlights	Ongoing throughout EGL	Internal communication	All employees	HR and team managers

TABLE 11.2 Sample recognition plan

Type of recognition	Eligibility	Type of reward	Details
Personalized appreciation	All EGL participants	Personalized appreciation messages	Personalized thank-you notes or emails from managers for EGL contributions
Monthly recognition meetings	All EGL participants	Team recognition, appreciation	Team meetings to celebrate EGL accomplishments and contributors
Peer-to-peer recognition	All employees	Peer recognition, appreciation	Nominations for exceptional EGL efforts by colleagues

Conditions

Evaluate the choices you made for the pilot. Is your software in place for content creation and learning sufficient? Do you need to scale it up? Do you need to extend it with better communication support? Do you need to track and trace learning results?

Assess your technology, budget and personnel; this may help uncover new ways to leverage your existing resources for EGL implementation.

Encourage cross-functional collaboration and knowledge exchange through new rules and processes.

Lastly, improve communication and recognition to scale EGL to new departments.

Creation

At this stage it's important to help authors create content and set up an easy system for organizing and storing knowledge. This way, the content will be both accessible and reader friendly.

A good way to help SMEs make learning material is to promote microlearning. It's simple to make, which is good for new authors. And when people find and use this information at work, they imme diately see its value. Encourage SMEs to capture lessons learned to facilitate continuous improvement to day-to-day processes.

A food delivery app in India wanted to keep a record of the lessons learned from their customer services team. However, they soon realized that simply recording these was not enough; they needed a systematic approach to apply the lessons effectively. During a retrospective meeting, they discovered that some lessons were repeated multiple times.

By identifying the repetition of specific lessons, the firm understood the significance of knowledge management. The core team incorporated the most recurring lessons into their future customer response guidelines, which prevented employees from repeating mistakes and enhanced customer support.

Ensure the SMEs feel responsible for keeping their content current and that their names are displayed on the courses. This will have three benefits:

- Better-quality resources because employees are less likely to produce sub-par content with their names attached to it.
- Credits authors for their work and expertise, offering added motivation for creating content.
- Builds a feedback loop between authors and learners.

Throughout the creation stage, recognize and showcase well-performing content and its creators, per the recognition plan you devised during the advocacy stage. This will motivate SMEs and inspire new authors to join the EGL league.

Small firms can quickly implement a 'who's who' page (a corporate directory akin to *Yellow Pages*) to help employees find the right people to seek advice, learn from or collaborate with on a project.

Evaluation

Unlike large enterprises that have set processes and procedures, smaller firms can hold informal evaluations that are quicker and more agile. Based on the evaluation results, you will determine the feasibility and success of the pilot. Moreover, you can make improvements to your EGL execution, introduce new tools or, if necessary, discard unsuccessful elements.

Next, assess the content produced in the pilot to identify strengths and weaknesses. One low-cost method to capture feedback is collecting anecdotal evidence, such as employee success stories and grading the content.

Another important factor to evaluate is the time savings achieved thanks to EGL. To assess this:

- measure the reduction of repeated questions and lessons
- evaluate the time taken to answer these questions through lessons
- track the number of employees using these insights

- calculate the time employees save by referring to these insights
- compare the number of content authors to the number of employees using the content.

Evaluate all this information to decide on the next steps.

The operational phase

Strategy

EGL should be firmly rooted in your company by now. The key is ensuring its continued growth and sustained value. A dedicated EGL facilitator adds significant value in this phase. While not necessarily a learning expert, this person should have piloted EGL and possesses the right skills to guide the group towards its objectives.

Following a successful pilot, the pilot will transition into a roll-out phase and later the operational phase. However, if you're considering expanding EGL into areas differing from the pilot's objective, consider initiating a separate pilot for that while progressing the original objective to the roll-out phase. Your approach can have more than one EGL initiative operating in various phases.

Advocacy

Now it's less about promoting the concept and more about reinforcing the process, sharing success stories to validate the EGL investment and maintaining motivation.

- Share insights on content usage with team leaders during monthly meetings. This helps gauge what needs to be adjusted in the evolving knowledge base.
- Establish a constructive environment for these dialogues. Leaders familiar with EGL will contribute to discussions about resource allocation, sharing best practices and keeping the momentum alive.
- Provide training and support so that new departments can implement their own EGL initiatives.

- Recognize the outstanding enablers and creators for their contributions.
- Recognize the broader team, comprising employees from different levels and departments who offer feedback, propose fresh content concepts and identify what needs to be updated.

Conditions

Remain critical about the tools you use. Are they still the right tools as the initiative progresses? Do they support your goals in the best way? Make adjustments where necessary.

- Establish routines for employees to document and share knowledge; make this an integral part of organizational work routines.
- Set guidelines for responsible content creation and sharing to avoid confidentiality breaches and IT risk.
- Implement IT systems to support creators and admins in managing EGL content and processes.

Creation

In today's age, even smaller companies have a global footprint. Our smaller-sized company, with fewer than 200 employees, operates in 4 countries and has employees all over the world. This necessitates translation and localization efforts and it's vital to actively manage this, not assume it will handle itself. This is the stage where you need to start considering these aspects.

Evaluation

It's essential to keep stakeholders informed on progress to maintain funding and support. However, assessing the ROI for any learning initiative can be challenging. Here are some tips on what you can do and what is not possible.

First, always have a clear overview of all costs involved in EGL. This includes L&D time and effort, investments in purchasing and running the tooling, time spent by SMEs and other aspects that can differ in each organization.

Second, quantify the savings achieved through EGL. Look into the cost of external courses that can now be replaced by EGL content, prior costs for translating and localizing resources, and so on. Note that the savings accrued from creating courses faster and more affordably contribute to the ROI. You can assess this financial impact by examining a variety of courses that are different in size and subject. Compare the effort expended to create them with what it might have taken without SME involvement. The objective is to pinpoint average savings per course.

Quantifying the value derived from learning initiatives is even more complex. It's almost impossible to *directly* link a learning initiative to productivity. You come closest with performance support content. If you can determine (for example by interviewing users) the average time savings these tools offer, you can then attribute a tangible value to them. However, for structured courses, this remains an elusive goal.

If you're at the start of your corporate learning ventures, the savings might not cover the investment initially. Since the impact on performance is hard to measure, you will need to sell the story to your leadership. Sell the idea of creating content by SMEs (and how it's faster and cheaper than setting up a learning department), explain the importance of knowledge retention and building the corporate brain, and explain the opportunities for performance support.

IMPLEMENTING EGL IS A PROCESS, NOT AN EVENT

Implementing EGL is an ongoing journey rather than a one-off event. This chapter underscores the understanding that it's a continuously evolving process, one that you can steer and refine. This process demands careful nurturing to get the best results. It's also shaped by many factors such as company culture, size, employee demographics and the technological resources available.

It's important that you realize that implementing EGL is not as simple as purchasing tools and initiating the programme. Just as buying a ticket and boarding your plane is not your holiday experience, launching EGL is only the beginning of your journey. And you would do well with some support during this process. That is why, at Easygenerator, we not only have a support team that answers application or didactical questions, but also a customer success team that supports customers throughout the process. This is a very important element of success.

Ensuring adequate support for both your content creators and the individuals overseeing the process is crucial; they both require guidance throughout this journey. So, as you start your EGL journey, look beyond just the launch. Secure that essential support – whether through your vendor, engaging with a community to share insights, or enlisting someone well versed in the process. Prioritize this support structure.

Our growth, both as a company and in terms of our product, has been in parallel with our customers. We matured as they matured. In our product's early stages, users began with basic text and media functions during their pilots. As their needs evolved, we improved our product to support their growth on the EGL maturity cycle. For instance, we identified that certain clients required translations and multilingual content to spread EGL across various regions. This need was a significant roadblock in their efforts to scale EGL organization wide. In response, we integrated an auto-translate feature, facilitating their transition from pilot stages to fully fledged roll-outs. Similarly, we expanded our offerings from a text-based solution to now include a text-to-speech feature, which greatly aids our enterprise clients in achieving accessibility and moving towards the operational phase.

Our product's growth clearly stems from our customers' needs, guiding us to develop features that facilitate the full-cycle implementation of EGL. This growth is an ongoing process that continues to this day.

Note

1 Bhamidi, V and Spiro, K (2019) Learning models in startup tech firms should be 50 percent self-learning, 50 percent social learning. Available at: https://www. chieflearningofficer.com/2019/09/16/the-5050-learning-model/ (archived at https://perma.cc/M6ZQ-3G5F)

12

The future of
Employee-generated Learning

We're witnessing fundamental changes in our society; these changes will certainly have an impact on corporate learning. In this final chapter, we investigate the consequences and implications of Employee-generated Learning. What lies ahead? Where will we be five years from now? How can EGL address some of the issues we will face?

One of the main principles and underlying beliefs of EGL is the shift from top-down to bottom-up, both in society and in corporate learning. We believe this is one of the main drivers behind an emerging learning culture. The employees in your company are workers and learners at the same time. They will take responsibility for their learning and development. But it will go beyond that; we must take this one step further. Employees will also have to take responsibility for the learning and development of their peers. By creating and sharing learning and performance content, they become channels of knowledge transfer, aiding their colleagues in refining skills and enhancing job performance.

As we advance, the constant availability of information will be the norm and this also applies to the workplace setting. **For this information to provide real value, it needs to be very specific and completely fit within the context of *your* work at the very right moment.** Centralized learning departments can't produce this level of detail and accuracy. This kind of information can only be created (and maintained) by SMEs, which requires a culture of knowledge sharing.

FIGURE 12.1 A prediction of the EGL ecosystem in the near future

Having such pinpointed information on hand as you navigate your work is transformative. It indicates a new era, reshaping the workplace, boosting performance support and revolutionizing workplace learning. We stand at the brink of a new learning landscape that is radically different from the traditional top-down approach.

EGL in the near future

To give you a clear view of what we expect for the future, we'll guide you through each component we believe will make up a full implementation of EGL a few years from now.

Figure 12.1 is the enhanced EGL process that we foresee for the future. Next to the L&D department and the instructional designers, we've added the following elements:

- The stakeholders to the business side, who are C-level executives and the managers of your SMEs.
- The human resources team in parallel with L&D.

- We also go into a little more detail by illustrating the three components that deal with knowledge sharing: creating, scaffolding and enhancing. Each component is further divided into three processes. We will go over these later in the chapter.

For EGL to reach its full potential as we envision, it must be seamlessly incorporated into everyday business operations. Realizing this objective requires the unwavering support of key stakeholders. This integration is precisely why we've included HR in our overview. Knowledge sharing must transition from a supplementary activity to an everyday essential; it should become an intrinsic part of every role, encompassed in job descriptions and annual evaluations, and maintain prominence in every employee's daily tasks.

Herein lies HR's role. By weaving knowledge sharing into the organization's core performance management processes, HR can set the foundation for it to become the 'new normal'. This will be accomplished when every employee's job description and performance review connects to the culture of knowledge sharing.

The instructional designers still play a crucial role in this future ecosystem. They not only guide and mentor SMEs in crafting content but also shoulder the responsibility of generating educational material themselves.

The impact of artificial intelligence

We cannot talk about the future of learning, or any future for that matter, without taking a closer look at the impact of AI.

The essence of AI is the creation and development of machines and systems capable of tasks traditionally requiring human intelligence. At its core, AI aims to replicate human cognitive functions. Its tasks include understanding natural language, recognizing patterns, solving complex problems, making decisions and learning from experiences. To do these tasks, it uses algorithms, vast amounts of data and substantial computational power.

For a long time, the profound influence of AI on our society has been evident. The fact that it can understand natural language has made it universally accessible. The introduction of ChatGPT brought the capabilities of AI to the forefront, allowing everyone to witness its power first hand.

There is much debate around AI at the moment. People are discussing the benefits but also the potential dangers; many people are afraid of what AI might do. There's a fear that AI might herald a new era in which machines supersede human intelligence. Nonetheless, history has taught us that we cannot stop innovation and every breakthrough can lead to both good and bad. Rockets can propel us into space, but they can carry bombs. Nuclear power can be a source of clean energy or be used to create devastating weapons. We not only know that we cannot stop innovation, we also know that the darker applications are inevitable. And while we might be powerless in curbing AI's negative potentials, we certainly possess the capability to amplify its positive ones. In our view, we need to tip the scales by maximizing AI's positive contributions and make sure that its benefits outweigh the threats.

For learning and development, AI is a game-changer. It removes boundaries. It will disrupt the LMS and LXP markets and will play a key role in various aspects of content creation and distribution. From tools used by microlearning content creators to AI-driven coaching for authors, AI helps add context and structure to content. In addition, chat interfaces powered by AI offer on-demand solutions and answers. Now, let's explain at greater length exactly how AI will impact each process within the application of EGL.

The EGL ecosystem

The EGL ecosystem represents an environment that facilitates all the processes for the next-level implementation of EGL and corporate learning. Much like the learning technology ecosystem we described in Chapter 8, the EGL ecosystem doesn't need to comprise one program from one vendor; it can be made up of many parts.

Central to the EGL ecosystem is the corporate brain, playing a crucial role in the future vision of EGL. It ensures that knowledge is long-lasting and readily available for anyone who needs it.

Creating

The creating part of the ecosystem comprises authoring, curating and collaborating. They form the creator environment that allows SMEs to capture their knowledge and experiences in the form of a formal course or training. On occasion, content will be crafted collaboratively by multiple SMEs or in tandem with instructional designers. Predominantly, however, SMEs will produce microlearning materials.

AUTHORING

The journey begins with the creators – the SMEs who possess the vital knowledge and share it using a creator platform. As we have mentioned throughout the book, **the emphasis in the future will be on creating microlearning rather than on courses or modules.** In fact, we anticipate over 90 per cent of all content created on these platforms will be microlearning, targeting workplace support. This content will encompass short instructional guides, tips and tricks, how-tos, checklists, FAQs, best practices and other similar content types. To facilitate this, you need a simple creator platform with no learning curve, allowing your SMEs to capture your knowledge through various mediums such as text, image, video or speech. The foundation for these capabilities already exists in creator platforms, but they need significant improvement.

Moreover, for a more holistic knowledge-sharing environment, we must expand the demographic of those involved in EGL. As of now, most contributors are white-collar professionals working at computers. We need to include all workers in this knowledge sharing. We must also consider blue-collar workers – like factory workers, construction professionals, truck drivers and others – who don't operate behind desks. For them, it's crucial to provide mobile platforms that prioritize microlearning and enable content creation through speech-to-text, audio and video. The ultimate goal is an inclusive knowledge-sharing environment, engaging everyone as both contributors and recipients.

> I (Kasper) have a hearing aid because I have a condition called tinnitus, a form of hearing damage. Recently, I upgraded to Bluetooth-enabled hearing aids that sync with my phone. With built-in speakers and microphones, these aids transform my phone into a hands-free device. They also feature a button which I programmed to initiate a query with ChatGPT and I hear the response directly in my ears, all without even touching my phone. Experiencing this was an eye-opener for me: connecting to a source of knowledge this easily, almost without any barrier, is incredible. It gave me a glimpse of the world of support waiting around the corner for people who don't work from behind a computer.

Another important area of improvement for creator platforms is that they must actively aid authors in content creation. Aside from offering a simple, intuitive and mobile-friendly UI, they must also integrate didactical and instructional design coaching. This includes helping authors decide what content to share and in which form to share it. Assistance in instructional design, writing, translation, design (among others) can now be achieved using a blend of rule-based engines and AI. A defining characteristic of AI is its ability to learn. An AI coach would refine and improve its coaching methodologies based on interactions with SMEs.

Since a large portion of formal learning content is generic, AI is already proficient in producing such content, whether it's courses or training, and this proficiency will only get better. This will directly challenge the traditional role of L&D. AI will soon serve as an instructional designer's assistant, presenting them with an advanced starting point for their courses.

The synergy of the corporate brain and AI will also impact the creation of courses that contain specific information. Imagine that the corporate brain contains the combined knowledge and experience of the SMEs on a topic. With AI, the instructional designer can extract this information from the corporate brain as a raw course. AI can enable instructional designers to extract this as a foundational course material. There's no longer a need to interview SMEs for content – they transition into a reviewing role. Taking it a step further, AI could autonomously craft a course, based on the insights of SMEs. Diving into this idea, the SME's primary role becomes filling the corporate brain with knowledge and keeping that information up to date. If that is the case, there is a good foundation for workplace support and creating specific learning material. The AI engine could automatically update courses created based on this information by either an SME or an instructional designer. When a piece of root information in the corporate brain is changed, AI can flag this content in courses or even change it for you. Imagine what this means. You would not only have an up-to-date source for workplace learning, you would have a guarantee that all learning content was always up to date.

If established, it lays a solid groundwork for workplace support and tailored learning material creation. An AI engine could automatically refresh courses based on this reservoir of knowledge. When core information in the corporate brain changes, AI can identify, flag or even adapt the related content in courses. Imagine what this means – not only will it produce real-time workplace learning but it also guarantees that every piece of learning content remains current.

CURATING

We believe there needs to be more emphasis on curating content. The curated content might range from general knowledge sourced from the broader web to specialized content originating within your organization. As we look into the future, AI tools will be instrumental in gathering content from these various sources. However, **we view AI as a supportive technology that should not take over the content creation or even take curation process away from people.** An AI system's accuracy depends on the quality of data it's supplied with. For instance, ChatGPT might occasionally provide incorrect answers, not due to technological inadequacies but because of inconsistent or inaccurate data from the web. This principle extends to corporate content. The reliability of AI-driven responses is directly tied to the quality of the initial content fed into the system. If the content is carefully curated from the beginning, the need for human oversight diminishes. Officially approved documents, for instance, can be incorporated without additional scrutiny. However, when dealing with uncurated sources, human curators play an essential role in determining the content's suitability for support, learning or even deciding whether it should be included in the corporate brain at all.

COLLABORATING

Collaboration is key for problem solving, innovation and effectively creating and sharing learning material. There are several reasons for this. First, content created by multiple people is often better than that created by a lone author. The very process of exchanging insights and challenging each other's perspectives naturally elevates the quality of the final output. Second, multiple contributors bring varied viewpoints to the table. This diversity prevents the dangers of tunnel vision and combines viewpoints to forge more comprehensive solutions. Furthermore, the journey of collaboration isn't just about the end result, it provides a profound learning experience where SMEs learn from each other. Where AI has a role to play is in helping to prevent redundancy by identifying duplicate content topics. More significantly, it also has the potential to connect experts sharing similar interests.

Scaffolding

The scaffolding process is designed to support employees in the flow of work. This is where they access workplace support, undergo learning and receive coaching.

LEARNING

In this context, we mean formal learning: a classroom session, a training, an e-learning module or a course delivered in a classroom or via an LM, LXP, intranet or other tools.

The potential disruption AI brings to this sector can be likened to its transformation of search engine methodologies. Where a traditional search engine directs you to a link, requiring you to delve in further for an answer, tools like ChatGPT give you the answer straight away. The majority of the learning and support software we have today operates in the manner of these traditional search engines: if you pose a question or seek knowledge, they point you towards a course, microlearning resource or other material that may hold your answer. But you're still tasked with extracting the answer yourself. Contrast this with the immediacy of AI, which delivers the answer the moment you ask.

When we succeed in applying this to performance support – when we can integrate AI to the interface of the corporate brain – it will revolutionize learning and performance. Think of a learning interface like ChatGPT as opposed to a search-driven one. It will change how people learn and develop and have a tremendous impact on our current learning environments like LMSs and LXPs.

COACHING

Within the EGL framework, it's the SMEs who are the primary contributors to the corporate brain. They're the ones answering questions from workers and devising solutions for ever-evolving challenges. Take this concept a step further and these SMEs can transition into roles of workplace coaches. Where providing the answer to a worker is asynchronous, coaching is synchronous.

We firmly believe that no matter how advanced technology becomes, it will never surpass the value of human interaction. Experienced workers, while valuable on their own, would have an even bigger impact on your organization if they would teach less experienced workers. This is the ultimate step in implementing EGL and developing a knowledge-sharing culture: SMEs working with newer employees, imparting their wisdom and insights, while also gaining fresh perspectives. This mutual exchange is pivotal not just in transferring knowledge but also in creating the next generation of SMEs, ensuring knowledge continuity beyond merely the digital corporate brain.

SUPPORTING

The notion of a corporate brain brings to life the sentiment expressed by Lewis Platt: 'If only HP knew what HP knows, we'd be three times more productive.'[1] (As we also shared in the preface of this book.) At any given moment, an employee could tap into this knowledge source to enhance their work, making every task more efficient.

AI-based solutions have the capability to pull the information from the corporate brain and present it to workers at the right time. They can even predict problems or questions and offer solutions *before* the need arises. This way, we would not solve problems faster but prevent them from arising. As Benjamin Franklin once said, 'An ounce of prevention is worth a pound of cure.'[2]

Though this may seem like a far-off future, but it's closer than we think. Contextual tools are already in use today. For instance, context-sensitive online help within software adjusts its guidance based on the user's current activity. Similarly, our phones, using GPS and proximity to mobile phone towers, provide real-time location-based insights. While it's undeniable that we're constantly under surveillance, such monitoring also brings its own set of advantages.

This support can go beyond tips, tricks, procedures and solutions and revolutionize decision making in the corporate world. All corporate decisions are (or should be) based on data and facts. How many times have decisions been stalled due to unresolved questions? With immediate answers at your fingertips, decisions would become swift and data driven.

Meanwhile, generic AI solutions like ChatGPT can complement company-specific information from the corporate brain with broader, albeit generic, insights. So, the ideal workplace support solution interface would pull precise answers from the corporate brain while also offering a general perspective from public AI sources. For example, if you ask a question on privacy legislation, the corporate brain might offer company-specific guidelines, while a public AI source could provide additional context. The combination of the two promises a wider understanding for the worker.

Enhancing

The final part of the EGL ecosystem is where innovation happens, where missing content is created and incorrect or incomplete content is improved.

SOLVING

Employees usually ask experts directly for help, whether in person, through chat platforms like Microsoft Teams or by email. The challenge with this approach is its one-on-one nature. While the person asking gets their answer, this helpful information isn't shared with others who might have the same question.

However, the new EGL setup proposes a shift. Instead of just giving the answer, the idea is to save this knowledge and add it to the corporate brain for everyone to use. While software can help with this, even a simple rule asking experts to save these insights can make a difference. AI can help by connecting information across the company. For example, if one department solves a problem, AI can suggest this solution to another department facing the same challenge.

Moreover, imagine a situation where you're working and face a problem or have a question. Almost immediately, the corporate brain chimes in with an answer or solution drawn from its vast repository. If, however, this brain doesn't house the required information, the system sends the question to a group of experts. Once they give a solution, it's sent back to the person who asked. After checking, this new information is added to the corporate brain. So, the next time someone has a similar question, the answer is already there.

IMPROVING

When an employee identifies that information from the corporate brain is not accurate or lacks details, they should have an option to mark it for review. Once flagged, this information should be directed to a specialized team of SMEs. These experts would then evaluate the flagged content, ensuring it's either validated as accurate or enhanced as needed. By maintaining this feedback loop, the corporate brain keeps improving and becomes more comprehensive.

INNOVATING

SME groups aren't only there to maintain and validate content, they're vital for innovation and fresh approaches. In many organizations, when there's a need for enhancement or a novel idea, a select group of experts is convened to brainstorm solutions. For instance, if the corporate brain fails to answer a worker's question, it triggers the SMEs to generate new content. Similarly, if an SME questions the validity of certain content in the corporate brain, it undergoes a rigorous review and is corrected, if required.

However, these expert groups should not be ad hoc or temporary. They shouldn't just convene when there's a specific challenge or issue. Instead, they should operate as a consistent entity. We believe that SMEs should be encouraged to collaborate regularly, exchanging insights and building on each other's expertise. If you mobilize this group only when a specific challenge arises, it's a reactive approach, akin to traditional learning mechanisms. But by fostering a constantly active group of experts, a proactive stream of new ideas, improvements and suggestions can emerge. They may even conceptualize solutions and innovations that wouldn't have been considered otherwise. For any organization aiming to evolve and expand, this kind of uninterrupted idea exchange is invaluable. It transforms a company into a dynamic entity, constantly adapting, growing and innovating.

The corporate brain

So far in this book we've discussed the corporate brain at great length. It's where the content from all eight EGL functions is stored, organized, contextualized and retrieved.

It's always been a challenge to create accessible and ready-to-use content. However, you can achieve this by combining the EGL approach with the new technologies that have become available (like AI). To make information accessible, you have to contextualize the content. This means you must analyze, organize and tag the content based on a taxonomy. A taxonomy is a hierarchical classification system for categorizing and organizing content. Even if you haven't heard of taxonomies, you may be familiar with the Linnean Taxonomy, which describes the living world in a hierarchical structure of eight levels, from the broadest to the most specific.[3] Humans are classified in the Linnean Taxonomy as:

- Kingdom: Animalia
- Phylum: Chordata
- Subphylum: Vertebrata
- Class: Mammalia
- Order: Primates
- Family: Hominidae
- Genus: Homo
- Species: Homo sapiens.

Organizing and contextualizing content within the corporate brain is crucial. To ensure that content isn't merely stored but is also easily retrievable in the appropriate context, it must be systematically categorized. Just as every living thing on our planet can be classified and understood within its specific habitat and role, so we should be able to categorize information in the corporate environment. (And yes, applying this is as tedious as it sounds.) For example, a piece of learning can be categorized by:

- the person who created the content
- the processes and tasks for which the information is relevant
- the supporting tools where there's a connection.

Since tagging content through taxonomies is so labour intensive, organizations rarely do it. This is where AI will come in. Due to its capacity to understand natural language, AI can decipher context and retrieve relevant information when you ask it to. Whether the data within a corporate brain would suffice for comprehensive analysis and answers remains a question. If not, a taxonomy-based approach complemented by support is an alternative. It could even be that a blend of both techniques proves most effective.

All nine processes supported by the EGL ecosystem directly relate to the corporate brain:

- **Authoring:** All content created by SMEs will be integrated into the corporate brain. It may be segmented from courses, but it will be included.

- **Curating:** This step ensures that the corporate brain houses only the most relevant, accurate and current content, knowledge and insights.

- **Collaborating:** Knowledge and insights from team collaborations often remain within that group. Through EGL, these insights are captured and shared across the corporate brain.

- **Learning:** The corporate brain may not host entire courses, but it will include information extracted from them, as well as microlearning developed directly by SMEs.

- **Coaching:** Insights derived from coaching sessions should be documented in the corporate brain, benefiting a broader audience.

- **Supporting:** The main purpose of the corporate brain is to aid workers in real time, enhancing their performance.

- **Solving:** This function addresses any gaps in the corporate brain.

- **Improving:** Update or rectify any content in the corporate brain that might be outdated or incorrect.

- **Innovating:** Valuable knowledge is gained during process improvements and innovation. Making this information available in the corporate brain ensures widespread access.

Learning has come full circle

Through the processes listed, SMEs support each other. Through coaching in particular, SMEs emerge as the modern-day masters, guiding the newer workforce – their apprentices. This makes a full circle to pre-1800 learning, bringing us back to the guilds' master–apprentices system. The younger generation, with their unique

FIGURE 12.2 The development of corporate learning

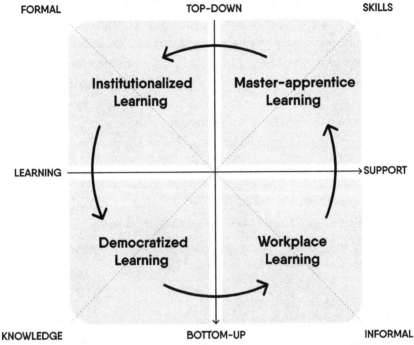

backgrounds, experiences and insights, also educate their seniors. The coaching and learning will now be reciprocal. This evolution of corporate learning over the last two centuries is illustrated in Figure 12.2.

In the 1800s, competency development was achieved through apprentices learning under masters. This was the core of learning in the medieval guild system and the root of workplace learning. With the Industrial Revolution came corporations, leading to structured corporate learning. This was also the birth of corporate learning and learning content creation. Learning shifted from a hands-on approach to a more documented one. The L&D department centralized learning, marking a transition from the traditional master–apprenticeship to a formalized structure. When we look at Figure 12.2, this transition moved corporate learning (institutionalized learning) from the top right quadrant to the top left one.

EGL was introduced to enhance and improve the content development of formal courses. **As SMEs became more involved in creating**

learning content, formal courses were replaced by knowledge sharing. On top of that, this led to the creation of niche content tailored for specific audiences, which traditional L&D approaches couldn't offer. The resulting democratization in content creation, knowledge sharing and EGL marked a paradigm shift to the bottom left quadrant (democratizing learning). This move is the main driver behind the success of EGL.

In recent years, SMEs have been generating content not just for learning but also for immediate workplace support in the form of microlearning. This evolution brings learning to the bottom-right quadrant (workplace learning). Finally, having the SMEs in a coaching role – much like the masters of before – brings us full circle, back to the top-right quadrant (master–apprentice learning).

Notes

1 Sieloff, C G (1999) 'If only HP knew what HP knows': the roots of knowledge management at Hewlett-Packard, *Journal of Knowledge Management*, 3 (1), 47–53. https://doi.org/10.1108/13673279910259385 (archived at https://perma.cc/6XS6-GE9W)

2 Supposedly, Franklin sent an unsigned letter to his own newspaper, *The Pennsylvania Gazette*. Published on 4 February 1735, his letter, 'Protection of Towns from Fire', began with the expression 'an ounce of prevention is worth a pound of cure'.

3 Von Linné, C, 1707–1778. *Systema Naturae*. Ed. 10., 1759. *Tomus II: Vegetabilia. Facsimile*, Weinheim, New York: J Cramer; Stechert-Hafner Service Agency, 1964.

AFTERWORD

Throughout the ages, sharing knowledge has remained a constant thread woven into the fabric of our society. Whether it was the early cave drawings depicting wisdom about animals and dangers to the next generation, or farmers passing down agricultural techniques to their kin, the act of knowledge sharing has been central to our evolution. Monarchs used to meticulously document history to preserve their legacy. Then the Industrial Revolution introduced new learning methods, with apprentices training under masters. Yet while the essence of knowledge sharing remains unchanged, the methods by which we access, distribute and use this knowledge have undergone profound transformations. The role of technology has been pivotal in this shift.

At the heart of this evolution lies the concept of EGL. This approach empowers anyone to share their insights, skills and expertise. Though it operates predominantly in an asynchronous manner, its full potential is unveiled when combined with synchronous modalities, like expert-driven coaching.

In our tech-centric world, the significance of human connection and understanding becomes even more evident, especially when helping employees learn and grow. Amid the digitalization of knowledge, the human aspect remains crucial. In this context, the role of authors and creators is invaluable. Equipping them with practical tools to create content, and establishing user-friendly systems to organize and store knowledge, becomes crucial. This ensures that knowledge is easily accessible and inviting for workers and learners. By merging human connection and creativity with the capabilities of modern AI, we pave the way for a more enlightened world in which knowledge knows no boundaries and is readily accessible to anyone with a thirst for learning.

Remarkably, for the first time, technology isn't a barrier, it's an enabler. We have the means to fully realize this vision. We know the direction, we have the bandwidth and the capability to connect everyone. The only thing that can stop us from unleashing the hidden power of employees in any organization is a lack of imagination and perseverance.

INDEX

Page locators in *italics* denote information contained within a Table or Figure.

Looking for another book?

Explore our award-winning
books from global business
experts in Human Resources,
Learning and Development

Scan the code to browse

www.koganpage.com/hr-learning-
development

Also from Kogan Page

ISBN: 9781398602625

ISBN: 9781398603103

ISBN: 9781398609129

www.koganpage.com

Printed in the USA
CPSIA information can be obtained
at www.ICGtesting.com
JSHW012304200224
57743JS00002B/12